NOW
NO OPPORTUNITY WASTED

8 WAYS TO CREATE A LIST
FOR THE LIFE YOU WANT

PHIL KEOGHAN
HOST OF THE DISCOVERY CHANNEL'S

with WARREN BERGER

RODALE

© 2004 by Phil Keoghan and Warren Berger

Back jacket photo credits (left to right): Claudia Pellarini; Patricia Lanza; Dan Farnam; Dan Farnam; Brooks Peterson; Patricia Lanza; Phil Keoghan; Claudia Pellarini; Dan Farnam; Kelsey Mazeur

Printed in the United States of America
Rodale Inc. makes every effort to use acid-free ∞, recycled paper ☺.

Book design by Christopher Rhoads

Library of Congress Cataloging-in-Publication Data

Keoghan, Phil (Phil John)
    No opportunity wasted : 8 ways to create a list for the life you want / Phil
Keoghan with Warren Berger.
        p.   cm.
    ISBN-13 978–1–59486–086–7 hardcover
    ISBN-10 1–59486–086–6 hardcover
    ISBN-13 978–1–59486–404–9 paperback
    ISBN-10 1–59486–404–7 paperback

    1. Self-actualization (Psychology)   2. Adventure and adventurers.   3. Risk-taking
(Psychology)   4. Lists—Miscellanea.   I. Berger, Warren.   II. Title.
BF637.S4K47   2004
158.1—dc22   2004017569

Distributed to the trade by Holtzbrinck Publishers

    4 6 8 10 9 7 5   hardcover
2 4 6 8 10 9 7 5 3 1 paperback

RODALE

WE INSPIRE AND ENABLE PEOPLE TO IMPROVE
THEIR LIVES AND THE WORLD AROUND THEM

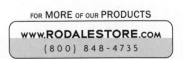

CONTENTS

ACKNOWLEDGMENTS

This book couldn't have happened without the unwavering support of a core group of people who believed in it—starting with the person who first uttered the words "No Opportunity Wasted." She is my best friend, fellow adventurer, business partner, and wife, Louise Keoghan. Thank you for providing endless cups of tea to keep me going, for always listening, and for helping me get around the rugged rocks. I continue to learn from you constantly. And to my beautiful and fearless daughter Elle, thanks for inspiring me every day.

Warren Berger is responsible for bringing the N.O.W. idea to life in this book, and also for giving me a voice on paper. I cannot say enough about his extraordinary ability to clarify my thoughts and ideas while adding new ones of his own. I am also indebted to Sloan Harris, my agent at ICM. When we were having early difficulties convincing publishers to gamble on this book, Sloan never wavered. He told me at the time: "Getting this book published is on my own personal N.O.W. list."

Thanks to my parents for teaching me the true meaning of N.O.W., and to Annette and Michael Grant for giving Louise and me a home in New York, and to Oprah Winfrey for letting me share my stories on TV. Also, Gary Brown, Babette Perry, Ira Schreck, Billy Campbell, Joe Abruzzese, Alix Hartley, Kristin Miller, Don Buchwald, Les Moonves, Ghen Maynard, Peter Faiman, Peter Howden, Peter Pistor, Michael Stedman, Bertram Van Munster, and the Greenbergs, my American grandparents. Finally, thank you to all the N.O.W. dreamers who agreed to be a part of this book. You are an inspiration to all of us, and I know your stories will encourage others to seek more from life.

—PHIL KEOGHAN

I first met Phil Keoghan at a diner in New York. I was assigned by *The New York Times* to interview him about a new TV show he was hosting, *The Amazing Race*. We subsequently returned to that diner many times over the next two years, to discuss the possibility of turning Phil's life-affirming experiences and philosophy into a book that could inspire others. We knew we were onto something when, during one of our brainstorms, a woman from a nearby booth came over. She said that listening to us had stirred in her a desire to start pursuing dreams she'd been postponing. Wherever that woman is today, I hope she fulfilled those dreams. I also hope she comes across a copy of this book. If she's reading it now, thank you.

Thank you to our editor at Rodale, Zach Schisgal. Special thanks to my loving and supportive parents, and to the Berger family—which lost a precious member last year when my wonderful brother Bill died suddenly at age 56. It was one of those too-painful reminders that life can be snatched from us at any time and must never be taken for granted (which, in essence, is the point of this book). Following Phil Keoghan's great advice and example, I am now compiling my own List for Life. Thanks, Phil, for sharing the N.O.W. philosophy with me, and thank you for your generous spirit and infectious enthusiasm. Finally, I wish to thank my hiking partner, my artistic muse, my most trusted reader and advisor, and the love of my life. These are all one person and I'm married to her. There is no opportunity, no adventure, and not even a single moment that I would ever wish to experience without Laura Kelly beside me.

—WARREN BERGER

1

WHAT IS *NO OPPORTUNITY WASTED?*

I AM UNDERWATER and in the dark, stranded somewhere deep in the bowels of a sunken ship that lies abandoned at the bottom of the sea. At the moment, I don't know which way is up or down. Inside a watery cavern that was once this ship's ballroom, my body is suspended sideways; the only thing that keeps me from free-floating is that I'm hanging on to the side of an anchored table by my fingertips. In the not-too-distant past, before this luxurious ship sank to the floor of the sea, this table was probably a spot where passengers shared cocktails and conversation. Must've been swell. But now it's just me, hanging on for dear life. I am beginning to wonder if this could be the end. I'm 19 years old.

I try not to panic. If I get too excited, my breathing will become irregular, and this will cause more problems with the regulator on my scuba air tank (I've already sucked in a few mouthfuls of salty water). I'm painfully aware that I have a finite amount of air in that tank, and that every minute I stay here, clinging to the table, is another minute lost. Should I be using these precious minutes to try to swim my way out of here? Maybe. Except I have no idea where to go. The inside of this ship is a labyrinth—all watery passages of indistinguishable gray silt walls, everything looking the same in the darkness. I would get more lost trying to navigate that maze. So I'm just staying put for now, hoping that help is on the way.

In the meantime, I'm alone with my thoughts. And they are not pleasant ones. For example, I am becoming extremely conscious, for the first time in years, of the claustrophobia I first felt years earlier, as a small boy. My mind flashes on an old image: the dark inside of a box, held over me by a couple of my young pals. They were just fooling around, but inside the box I was overcome with terror, flailing my arms against the cardboard until the boys let me out. Of course, everything was fine once the box was lifted; I laughed it off with everyone else. My current situation, unfortunately, is more worrisome.

The mind races at times such as these. Mine is filled with not just memories and fears, but questions. First and foremost: How the hell did I ever get myself into this mess? The only answer—it's not a good one, I know—is that it's hard for a 19-year-old to resist an adventure, especially when it's part of his job. I'd just landed a dream gig working on a local New Zealand adventure TV show, and this happened to be one of my assignments: to dive down to where a sunken cruise ship lay abandoned, the waterlogged remains of a terrible accident 2 years earlier that had forced people in elegant evening attire to jump ship.

Before this dive, I was giddy with anticipation. The 22,000-ton behemoth promised to be a kind of lost world, untouched and unseen by the public since the calamity had occurred. I was also undeniably nervous. I'd never done anything like this and wasn't sure how well I'd take to being underwater, in the dark, and in a confined space. To make matters worse, I wasn't qualified to do a dive like this, didn't have a safety line, and didn't even have proper light sources. None of this stopped me from strapping on scuba gear and diving right in, following close behind another diver from the salvage crew.

We swam down 20, then 60, then 100 feet. Gradually, I caught sight of the massive ship, lodged on its starboard side in the ocean floor. It was breathtaking. I'd have been content to swim around studying the exterior of the shipwreck, but the diver I was following—one of the only people who'd been inside the sunken ship previously—quickly swam toward a small open porthole, lunged through it, and vanished into the ship. Without hesitating, I followed him down that hole.

Soon we were gliding through the liquid corridors of the ship. It was dark, but with the light of our flashlight we glimpsed a strangely beautiful world, embalmed in a monochrome film of silt. We swam into the ship's ballroom, where much of the interior remained intact but was now turned sideways—including the tables and chairs still bolted to the floor and a crystal chandelier that swayed from what was once the ceiling. I noticed floating suitcases and wondered what was inside them.

We were supposed to wait there in the ballroom for an underwater camera crew to join us. As we settled in to wait, my fellow diver signaled to switch our lights off to save battery power, and everything went pitch-black. Time passed as we bobbed silently in the cold and eerie darkness. The camera crew didn't show up.

We weren't sure what to do. Should we look for the camera crew? Maybe they were lost. At that point, we made the mistake of splitting up—the other diver went off to look for the crew, while I stayed behind to see if they would show up. It didn't take long for me to realize that I was in a very vulnerable situation now: I had a limited air supply, and no idea where I was in this ship. I don't know how long I was alone like that. But I know that at a certain point in time, the aloneness, the uncertainty, the darkness, the quiet, and the claustrophobia all came together and had a powerful effect on me. For the first time in my life, I felt the grip of panic.

Which brings me back to where I began this story: hanging on, and trying not to think too much. And yet I couldn't stop thinking . . . I thought of possibilities and scenarios, some hopeful and some bleak. I was riding a kind of emotional seesaw: One moment I was up high, reassuring myself that "it's okay, someone will show up soon, just stay calm." The next moment, I felt myself descending to the bottom of the seesaw, the dark side where reason gives way to panic, and where doubt (*"How do you know anyone's coming back?"*) overrides faith. Gradually, the seesaw became unbalanced, with fear outweighing all else. And along with fear, what was slowly seeping into my mind was a feeling of regret. What if it did all end here—with me pathetically clinging to this little table (I can even imagine the absurd headline: *"Man Drowns in Shipwreck—Two Years Later!"*). What if I never got to do all the things I'd been planning to do—all those crazy things I'd dreamed about while growing up? If it's hard to say goodbye to the life you've lived, it's even harder to say goodbye to a life you have yet to live. But I was beginning to say that farewell—the seesaw was down for good, it seemed—when everything started to cloud up and dissolve. And what came next was . . . nothingness.

THIS EXPERIENCE happened 17 years ago. I parted ways with the conscious world on that day, though not permanently. Sometime later— I cannot tell you how much time passed—I opened my eyes and found myself back in the world of light and air and living color. Concerned faces peered down at me as I lay on my back gasping, safely on the deck of the salvage boat. The other diver had indeed come back and found me, though I never saw him arrive. I shudder to think of the condition he found me in. I now know, from talking to experts who rescue people trapped in caves, that I had probably reached the final stages of survival, at which point the mind shuts down and pure animal instinct takes over.

It's quite possible I clawed and scratched on those silt walls around me, trying to get out. But I'll never know for sure, because I have no memory of those last desperate moments before my rescue.

What has stayed with me to this day, however—and will for the rest of my life, I'm sure—is the experience of coming face-to-face with my own mortality. It changed me, immediately and profoundly. It gave me a sense of urgency, a hunger for life, that many people don't feel until they're approaching the actual, irreversible end of their lives. It is only then that so many of us finally arrive at a reckoning point and ask: "*What must I do before I die?*"

But I started asking that question at the ripe old age of 19—practically from the moment I opened my eyes on that rescue boat and looked up at a life that had been given back to me. I've been asking the question, again and again, ever since. And I keep writing down the answer, in the form of a list.

I began compiling that list of "things to do before I die" the same day that I was rescued. The first version of the list was written on the back of a brown paper lunch bag, in pencil, with words scribbled in and crossed out—the handwriting of someone in a hurry to start living. I don't have that original list anymore, but I remember what was on it, and I particularly recall what was at the top of the list. I wasted no time in doing that thing. That very afternoon, I strapped my scuba gear on again and swam back inside the shipwreck to complete my original assignment—after which I checked off what I'd written at the top of my list. Somehow I just knew that my list, and my new life, had to start with going back to that place where I'd felt so afraid. I didn't want to live with that fear always in the back of mind, so I went down and faced it. (Oh, and I stayed with my diving partner this time; I may have been foolish, but I was no fool!)

From that day on, I kept adding to that handwritten list, giving myself more challenges to conquer, more dreams to pursue. Once I wrote something down, there was never any question in my mind that I would turn it into a reality. Following that list, or rather propelled by it, I set out on a series of life adventures that have led me into primitive jungles, up to the highest mountains, and down to the bottom of the ocean (where all this got started). My ever-changing list demanded that I hurl myself from a tower with a cord tied to my feet, feed killer sharks by hand, romp around au naturel at a nudist colony, swim from Europe to Asia, and stay overnight in an "ice hotel" in Finland.

PHIL'S LIST FOR LIFE
(Age 19)

The first list I ever made up was handwritten on the back of a brown paper bag. I'd almost drowned, and this filled me with a sense of urgency about life. The first thing on my list was to go back underwater and conquer that frightening experience, so I could move on to others. A lot of the things I wrote down on that early list involved thrill-seeking, and I've since come to understand what was going on. I was looking for a way to replicate that "rush" of coming face-to-face with death. It seems crazy, but when you have an episode like that, you come out feeling more alive than ever before. For a while, I almost became hooked on trying to re-create that feeling through life-threatening stunts: I jumped, I dove, I strapped myself onto speeding objects. Eventually, I came to realize that there were many other ways to lead a fuller, more interesting life, without constantly risking my

Why did I feel a burning desire to do such things? All I can say is that something deep within me craved experiences like these. And I was convinced that each of these experiences would somehow enrich my life— which, in every case, proved to be true.

In many ways, my list became my life. It determined what I did and whom I met. It became a core part of my identity. And it led me to a career in which I was able to chase my own dreams and help others chase theirs, and all the while (believe it or not) get paid for it. I started out by producing and hosting adventure television programs in my homeland of New Zealand. It was a blast until, as is my tendency, I felt the urge to

---

neck. And I also came to appreciate that a good List for Life should be more mature, more emotionally rich, and much more varied than this one. (But hey, I was 19.)

1. Go back into that sunken ship. ✓
2. Dive the world's largest underwater cave. ✓
3. Hand-feed sharks. ✓
4. Climb Mount Everest.
5. Walk on the wing of a Tiger Moth biplane. ✓
6. Learn how to barefoot water-ski. ✓
7. Go bobsledding in Calgary. ✓
8. Scuba dive on the Great Barrier Reef. ✓
9. Get my skydiving license. ✓
10. Travel the world as a bartender on a cruise ship.
11. Get in the ring with a professional fighter. ✓
12. Fly on a rocket into outer space.

PHIL'S CURRENT LIST FOR LIFE
(Age 30-Something)

You'll notice I've scaled back on some of the climbing and jumping. And yet, I am proud to say, much of this list is still rather childish. Once you've made your own List for Life, don't hesitate to change it, add to it, adapt it: It should be a fluid and dynamic document. It should evolve as you grow. In terms of my own evolving list, my first one was very self-centered, as in, "I want to experience this, I want to see what it feels like to do that." I think one of the biggest differences over time is that now I tend to want to do more things that involve other people: meeting interesting people, immersing myself in a foreign culture, going with someone on a journey, helping someone to achieve a dream. I've found that the latter has become the ultimate "rush" for me because it makes me feel as if I've changed someone's life, and now maybe she will turn around and share her experience with someone else and change *that* person's life, and the whole thing will keep spreading (that's the plan, anyway).

The *No Opportunity Wasted* book and TV series are still at the top of my current list, with little check marks next to them. I may have given birth to both these babies, but I still feel like I'm just getting started in terms of bringing the N.O.W. movement fully to life.

move on and break new ground. In the early 1990s, I took a leap of faith and came to the United States with no prospects, naively thinking that surely some television network was bound to take an interest in an unknown fellow from Down Under who liked to dive and jump and ex-

1. Write the book *No Opportunity Wasted*. ✓
2. Produce the N.O.W. television show. ✓
3. Climb Mount Everest (don't worry, I'm getting to it).
4. But before that, climb Mount Cook with my dad, age 62.
5. Travel into outer space.
6. Be a ball boy in the U.S. Open.
7. Take an inner-city kid to the fields of Nebraska and create "crop art."
8. Take my daughter, Elle, to La Tomatina in Spain, the world's biggest food fight.
9. Find a way to help a guy I know named Jesse return to his beloved surfing, even though he is paralyzed.
10. Have a gourmet romantic dinner with my wife, Louise, on top of the erupting Stromboli volcano.
11. Take Oprah Winfrey skydiving, or something (she deserves it; plus, I owe her one for putting me on her show).
12. Complete the Hawaiian Ironman triathlon before I turn 40.
13. Finish training for my pilot's license and fly a small plane around the world.
14. Free-dive with 3,000 singing humpback whales off the coast of the Dominican Republic.
15. Have a barbecue at the South Pole.

plore. Incredibly enough, it happened—and in the years that followed, I took part in hundreds of on-camera adventures as host and producer of an internationally syndicated TV series called *Keoghan's Heroes* and then another series on the Discovery Channel called *Adventure Crazy*. After

OH, THE THINGS I'VE DONE!

- Played "speed golf" in the deadly Australian Outback
- Renewed my wedding vows underwater with a scuba-diving priest and a dolphin in attendance
- Changed a light bulb on top of New York's 700-foot Verrazanno Bridge
- Skied behind a reindeer at 30 miles per hour
- Slept in a tree in the Costa Rican jungle
- White-water rafted the Jordan River of Israel
- Set a world record for group bungee jumping
- Won a cow-patty throwing competition 174 feet (53 meters)!
- Was spiritually cleansed by a witch doctor in Asia's Golden Triangle
- Tracked a Florida panther through alligator-infested waters
- Went scuba diving with a dog
- Hunted a giant rat in the Venezuelan rain forest
- Drank cobra blood
- Won a spaghetti-eating competition (now *that* almost killed me)

that, the next leg of my journey took me around the world, as host of CBS's Emmy-winning *The Amazing Race*—a series of grueling-yet-exhilarating races spanning the globe in 36 madcap days.

But even a race around the world now seems like a modest quest compared with my newest adventure, which represents the biggest, most meaningful challenge of my life. It is called *No Opportunity Wasted* (or, for those who like to cut to the chase, N.O.W.). It is the basis of both a new television series on the Discovery Channel and the book you are holding in your hands. But more than anything else, *No Opportunity Wasted* is a philosophy and a way of life.

IN ESSENCE, *No Opportunity Wasted* is about learning how to live while you still have the chance, about letting go of the handrails, taking off your tie (and maybe taking off a lot more while you're at it), and swerving off that predictable road you've been following for years—onto a strange and bumpy path that just might, with a bit of luck, get you lost. It is about taking the time to enjoy experiences you've denied yourself. But it is also about sharing experiences with other people you know. And connecting with people you don't know. Beginning with yourself.

The philosophy is rooted in the notion that each of us must follow our many and varied dreams in order to lead a fuller, richer life. *But first we must figure out what those dreams are—and write them down on a list.* That's not something to be taken lightly. This book will help guide you as you create your own personalized, meaningful "List for Life." The goal of *No Opportunity Wasted* is not to put forth a rigid set of rules, a one-size-fits-all approach, or a generic list of "things that I think you should do with your life." I hold firmly to the idea that my List for Life is just for me, and your list—which perhaps you haven't written down yet but which exists nonetheless, etched in your soul—is entirely different from mine, and should be. While I dream of scaling Mount Everest, your quest may be to walk the entire way around New York City's Central Park in one afternoon. Indeed, you don't necessarily have to go halfway around the world to follow your dreams. Opportunities for unforgettable moments and deeply meaningful experiences are all around, if you open yourself up to them.

You can live a N.O.W. life without spending a lot of money. Imagi-

N.O.W. MOMENTS:
HOW MANY HAVE *YOU* HAD?

What is a N.O.W. moment? Think of it as an immortal memory. Something you did that stays with you. It makes you smile when you remember it, and you tend to tell others about it years later. It was a singular experience in your life. It needn't have been a momentous accomplishment. A friend recalls discovering a golf driving range in the Caribbean that faced out toward a beautiful ocean horizon. At sunset, he got himself a tropical drink in a plastic cup and spent the next glorious half-hour sipping his drink and driving golf balls into the golden setting sun.

That's a "N.O.W. moment," and he made it happen by being alert to the possibilities. Occasionally, such moments are handed to us by fate (the birth of a child, for example). But those are relatively rare. If you want more N.O.W. moments, you must shape and create them, using ordinary moments as your clay.

So let's take stock: How many immortal moments in your own life can you think of? Jot them down on a piece of paper. Take some time to think about this. Mull it over, and ask your friends and family if necessary. When you've exhausted your memory, see how many moments you have written down. And now ask yourself: Am I content with the number of N.O.W. moments I've had? If you've come up with, say, 10 moments, that doesn't seem too bad—except when you consider how many minutes you've lived in, say, the past 25 years (to be exact, that would be 13,148,640 minutes). So: Ten great moments out of 13 million—are you really happy with that ratio? Don't you think you can do better?

nation is your currency when it comes to acquiring great experiences. And you don't have to risk your life, either. This is an important point to emphasize, because people often assume that "adventure" is synonymous with extreme risk-taking. But my personal belief—and the philosophy of *No Opportunity Wasted*—is that "being adventurous" is really about taking mental leaps. It's about being willing to move beyond your comfort zone and try something different. And there are countless ways one can do that, most of which have nothing to do with jumping out of planes.

In fact, there are so many ways to experience the *No Opportunity Wasted* life, so many different possibilities to put on your own list, that the sheer abundance can be overwhelming. Having too many choices can make it hard to come up with a definitive list of things you want to do. And so one of the functions of this book is to help you sort through those endless possibilities, organize them, and categorize them. To that end, the book lays out eight categories or "universal themes," encompassing almost every type of experience imaginable. These themes address deep, basic urges that most of us long to fulfill in some way, such as the need to "face one's fear," to "express oneself," to "get lost," or to "test one's limits."

This book will focus on the featured themes, examine why they're deeply important to us all, and take a look at firsthand stories of how ordinary people have responded to these particular needs by trying something new and life-changing. Some of the people you'll meet here are referred to as the "N.O.W. dreamers;" these are some of the thousands of people who've submitted letters and applications describing their lifelong dreams to the *No Opportunity Wasted* television series. Those who were selected for the TV series were given a budget of

The Eight Great Themes

- Face Your Fear
- Get Lost
- Test Your Limits
- Take a Leap of Faith
- Rediscover Your Childhood
- Shed Your Inhibitions/Express Yourself
- Break New Ground
- Aim for the Heart

$3,000 and 72 hours to turn their dreams into reality (as you'll see, some of them truly made the most of that opportunity). Other people you'll meet in these pages are those I've personally helped as they've taken on fears or challenges. And still others are remarkable people who've inspired *me* during my travels and adventures around the world. But all the people have one thing in common: They're determined to live out their dreams.

In each of the theme chapters, once we've looked at how other people are pursuing great experiences, we'll then explore ways *you* can seek out a more personalized experience that ties in with that overall chapter theme. From wild to mild, we'll cover a broad range of possible experiences—with "milestones" designed to help you begin with small steps and build up to bigger ones. The book is structured to guide you step-by-step as you construct a List for Life that makes sense for you and truly speaks to *your* dreams.

AT THE END of each chapter, I'll ask you to do one easy but very important thing: Write down one ultimate experience that you'd like to pursue, inspired by the theme of that chapter. I'm even giving you an official List for Life work sheet on which to write. No, it's not a brown paper bag; it's your own detachable dream-list page, found in the back of the book. You'll notice that it's structured like a contract, because that's what it's meant to be—a sacred, binding agreement that you will make with yourself.

By the time you finish with the eight theme chapters (chapters 3 through 10), you should have an eight-point list filled in. But just in case you still need more ideas and inspiration, chapter 11 provides examples of complete lists filled out by a range of people from all walks of life. These people were asked, in advance, to create N.O.W. lists and then share their dreams with readers of this book. Among those who took us up on this offer are a top Hollywood agent, the chief executive of one of the best-known companies in advertising, a man battling a life-threatening illness, a woman beginning a new life as a retiree, a famous television actress, a nun who runs marathons, a soldier returning from Iraq, a schoolteacher, and an artist who spent much of his life in prison. The *No Opportunity Wasted* concept and philosophy resonated with each of these diverse individuals.

And that doesn't surprise me. As I've traveled around the world, taking some pretty remote trails along the way, I have encountered the spirit of N.O.W. almost everywhere I've gone. When I've shared stories about my own adventures and my philosophy with people, invariably something in them lights up, and then the secret comes out: *"I'd love to live that way myself."* Then they reveal to me that they've always wanted to stare into the eye of a whale, or "skeleton-ride"

(continued on page 18)

Are You a "N.O.W." or a "Nah" Person? Take the Official N.O.W. Survey

In my experiences on *The Amazing Race*, *Adventure Crazy*, and the *No Opportunity Wasted* television series, I've found that anyone can rise to the challenge of adventure. Old or young, man or woman, fit or unfit, calm or nervous—it doesn't make a difference. What does matter are attitude, imagination, desire, curiosity, and other intangibles that are found deep inside. Do you have what it takes? Take this "Yes/Nah" test and find out.

- You come home from work with a Blockbuster video. The phone rings. It's your crazy pal Louis, who has free tickets to some strange performing arts show wherein people cover themselves in chocolate. Do you go check it out?
- You're on your way home from the show, hungry for a late-night snack (anything but chocolate). You pass an odd-looking new restaurant, and of course Louis stops and looks in. Soon, the owner is explaining that the cuisine "is from Namibia with just a touch of Botswana." He hands Louis a sample appetizer that has many legs. Louis tries it and says, "It's fantastic," passing some to you. Do you give it a try?
- You've always wanted to travel to a remote part of the world, but you don't have the money. As you are grousing about this to an unsympathetic Louis, he yells, "Stop whining. If you really want to go, there are ways to do it on the cheap—but you have to be flexible. And willing to sleep in a tree." What do you say?

• You're hiking down a mountain on a beautiful sunny day, your back a bit stiff from sleeping in a tree. In the valley below, there's a stream you'd love to swim in, but it'll take hours to walk down there and the sun will have set by then. "Bummer," you grumble. Then your hiking companion (yes, it is Louis) stops and pulls a rope out of his backpack. "No worries," he says. "We'll just rappel down the side of the mountain." Do you take the rope?

• When you get to that beautiful stream, you realize you don't have a swimsuit. There are only three other people around—a couple of old guys fishing, and of course crazy Louis, who announces, "Gangway, because I'm going in bare-assed." Are you going in bare-assed, too?

Results: If you answered yes to at least four of the five questions, then you're definitely a N.O.W. person; think of this book as a handy program guide for a club of which you're already a proud member. If you got two or three yeses, you're a "kinda-N.O.W." person. You have loads of potential but need to kick it up a notch, and this book should do the trick. If you got only one or zero yeses, then I'm sorry to inform you that you are a "Nah" person. But don't despair: You have the most to gain from this book, the most potential for achievement and new experiences. You're to be envied in a way, because you have the opportunity to *completely change* your lifestyle, instead of just upgrading. Odds are you'll appreciate new experiences more than anyone—because you're starved for them, even if you don't know it. (Don't say nah. I'm telling you the truth!)

headfirst down an Olympic luge track, or trek through a rain forest accompanied by a dear old friend they haven't seen in years. I've encountered this yearning spirit in the macho corporate boardrooms of Wall Street, as well as in the predominately female studio audience of *The Oprah Winfrey Show*. I've found it among Hollywood stars and small-town store clerks, among teenagers, soccer moms, and retirees alike. It crosses all boundaries, because it is innately human. It is programmed into the stimulation-seeking D4DR gene on chromosome 11, which serves as "mission control" for the spirit of adventure. The urge to explore and to experience is hardwired in all of us.

But somewhere along the way, many of us have lost touch with that basic part of our nature: We've grown a little soft, predictable, comfortable. We've become trapped in routines, absorbed by the burdens of daily life. The author Tim Cahill has observed that most of us "abandon the idea of a life full of adventure sometime between puberty and the first job. Our dreams die under the dark weight of responsibility." Yes, it's true: We all have too little time to spare, too many jobs that need doing, not enough money in the bank, and a hundred other good excuses.

With that in mind, before starting on the theme chapters and the point-by-point construction of your list, we're going to first take care of a few little niggling personal matters, involving all those pressing responsibilities you have, and your various concerns about the kids, not to mention your exhausting work schedule, and of course that chronic bad back of yours that keeps flaring up. I am talking about, in a word, your *excuses*. They are the stumbling blocks that, for the moment, separate you from the *No Opportunity Wasted* life. And they will keep you from ever taking the first step, if you let them. If you truly desire a full

SAY HELLO TO "GENE WILD"

So you want to take a risk, try something different, live a little dangerously. Does this mean you're crazy? No, it may just mean you have a healthy and slightly elongated gene that goes by the number D4DR—or, as I like to call it, "Gene Wild." Genetic researchers working independently in Israel and the United States several years ago observed that people with a longer D4DR gene were more apt to seek out novelty and thrills. Here's why: The gene is a receptor for dopamine, a chemical messenger that can create the sensation of pleasure. If you have a longer D4DR gene, you need to absorb more dopamine in order to feel a "rush"—hence, you may feel the urge to push your own "panic button," engaging in thrilling activities partly to try to stimulate this chemical process.

It's quite likely Gene Wild helped our ancestors to survive in dangerous days of old, which is why the gene itself survived and was passed on to us. As Michael Aptor, Ph.D., noted in *Psychology Today* magazine, prehistoric folks who were adventurous and willing to take risks were better able to explore new territories and make new discoveries (such as finding and sampling edible foods), thereby benefiting their group. And their willingness to swing from a rope may have helped them to stay one step ahead of the predators.

life, then there is no room in it for excuses—you must simply clear them out. But they're tough little buggers that tend to hang on, so we're going to do our best to demolish them, one by one, in the next chapter.

OKAY, IT SOUNDS GOOD . . . BUT MUST I DO ALL THIS *NOW?*

Why is it so important to begin writing your list and embarking on your new life right away? After all, there's always "tomorrow". . . not to mention "someday," which is a good time to change your life, right? Wrong. If you're serious about changing your life, you *have* to do it now, and here is why.

- **Because now you can.** We're blessed to be living in a time of abundant opportunity and in a world that is more open and accessible to all of us than ever before. A life of rich and varied experience is now available to almost *anybody*, not just the elite wealthy or the die-hard globetrotters and adventurers. I'm now seeing people from all classes and walks of life participate in adventurous living because they can (the "adventure travel" industry has grown by leaps and bounds since the mid-1990s and has continued its surge, even after the September 11 tragedy). Previous generations didn't have those cheap Internet airfares, but more to the point, they didn't have the kind of freedoms we enjoy. For many, their time and effort was consumed by getting by—tilling the soil, working in a factory, making ends meet. My grandfather worked in a garage from sunup until he came home at night exhausted; a "special moment" in his life was when he was lucky enough to have a nice cup of tea before bed. Today, even the most hardworking among us have more vacation time, more freedom, more disposable income, more options. Travel is a regular part of our lives, and if we choose, we can go "off road" in a way that earlier travelers couldn't. Trails have been blazed for you in recent years, allowing you to venture out and explore with the knowledge that it has been done by others, safely. And you can go armed with *loads* of information, available at your fingertips—from books, Web sites, magazines. You can find out where to go, the coolest things to do when you get there, and how to save money on the way. You can share information with someone across the country who also likes to scuba dive in caves or bird-watch—and they can give you a few firsthand tips. All of this doesn't mean it's easy to live a N.O.W. life, but it's easier now than it was before. And maybe it's easier now than it will be in the future.

• **Because tomorrow, the world may change.** In fact, it most surely will. In fact, it already has. In these unsettling times of terrorism and war, some of the opportunities you take for granted today could be lost tomorrow. Your ability to travel freely to certain places could become restricted. Environments that were once welcoming may become less so. On top of that, factor in the effects of continuing global industrialization and the worldwide homogenization of cultures: It means you cannot assume that something beautiful and unique that exists right now will be the same tomorrow. Better get to that unsullied oasis in your dreams without delay—because you may look up one day and discover they've opened a Wal-Mart there.

• **Because your own capabilities and circumstances will change.** There are things you can do right now that you will not be able to do quite as well in 5 years (this is true whether you're 29 or 59). Which is not to discourage anyone from doing anything at

(continued)

(continued)

Must I Do All This *Now?*

any age; in this book, you'll meet people in their seventies and eighties who are fully embracing the N.O.W. lifestyle. But the fact is, you experience some things differently as a 30-year-old than as a 50-year-old—and you should not miss the chance to have *both* experiences. Along with physical changes, your life circumstances may also change in the future. As little "free time" as you have now, you may soon have even less because of something you cannot foresee at the moment.

• **Because probability diminishes as procrastination escalates, inevitably yielding a result that equals . . . nothing, squared.** Okay, I just concocted this formula myself, but I defy you to dispute the basic soundness of it: The longer we put off something we plan to do, the less likely it becomes that we will *ever* do it. Over time, a dream that is not acted upon becomes more remote, more unreal in our own mind, and more daunting. After enough time, we become intimidated and paralyzed by the things we have postponed and failed to act upon. It just gets harder and harder to break the inertia and take that first step. Also, over time, we build up more and more excuses and reasons not to do it. "Well, now I've got the mortgage and the kids—but wait 5 more years, then I'll be ready." Guess what: In 5 years, you'll have even more excuses available to you.

• **Because life is a gift . . . which unfortunately comes with an expiration date.** What's worse, that date is unknown. We've all heard the sad stories about people who planned to do something wonderful and then were suddenly, unexpectedly, derailed by illness. Recently, I got to know a professional diver named Shane Platt, who approached the N.O.W. television series because he wanted us to help him overcome his lifelong fear of sharks. He should've known what he'd be wading into when he came to us—before long he was in the water and surrounded by dull black eyes and sharp white teeth (did he survive? You'll have to read chapter 3 to find out). But the point I want to make here is that Shane felt an urgent need to tackle this fear, *immediately*. When I asked him why, he began to mention his parents. All their lives, they'd put things off, looking forward to a golden age retirement when they'd get to live out their own list of dreams. But then Shane's mother suddenly was diagnosed with cancer and died before she had a chance to do any of those things. This left Shane feeling determined "not to make the mistake my mother and father made," as he told me. In a way, Shane's experience with his parents affected him the way my own experience in the shipwreck affected me, and the way September 11 affected so many of us. Think of it as a ringing alarm from a clock that, like it or not, is ticking away and telling us that the time to act is *now*. So don't ignore it and put your head under the pillow. Get moving. You can start by turning the page.

2

FIRST STEP: GETTING RID OF EXCUSES

NO MORE "WOULDA-COULDA-SHOULDAS"

GEE, I DON'T KNOW if writing a book is such a good idea. I mean, there are 150,000 books published every year and that's too many already, so why add another to the heap? And besides, how am I going to write a book when I'm in the midst of producing a 13-episode television series for the fall 2004 TV season? I could get around to the book next year or the year after, but . . . get it done *this* year? I don't see how. Yes, I realize we've got a publisher who's ready and eager to do the book now, and that we may not have another opportunity like this. But I can't help thinking the best time for N.O.W. might be . . . later. After all, this is an *election year* (I'm not sure how that's relevant, but it must be). Also, though most of the people I've talked to about *No Opportunity Wasted* loved the idea, there was that *one guy* . . . you know, that tax attorney in New Jersey. Hated the idea. Thought we'd do better with a concept like *No Loophole Overlooked*. Who's to say he's wrong? And did I mention my right index finger has an incredible blister? It's true that my coauthor, Warren, will be the one at the keyboard much of the time, but if it should turn out that *I* have to do a lot of typing, there is *no way* I can do it with this finger.

If I had paid attention to any of the countless excuses available to me, the book you're holding in your hands would not exist. And perhaps neither would any other book on the shelf, because for every one of them there was an author who probably had to fight past many great reasons for *not* doing that book. How many book ideas—including some with the potential to become best sellers or even classics—must have died under the crushing weight of excuses? And it's not just books: Excuses smother ideas and dreams and goals of every form and shape. They jeopardize anything that is ambitious or challenging; anything that carries with it a little risk; and, most of all, anything that is not absolutely mandatory (after all, you don't really *have* to write that book or climb that mountain or lead a fuller life. And you certainly don't have to do it *now*, do you?).

Through nearly 2 decades of trying to encourage, prod, inspire, or sometimes just pester people into doing more with their lives, I've encountered every excuse imaginable—though people are always capable of surprising me with new ones. I actually take pleasure in listening to people make up their excuses, because it reveals how creative they can be. If people put as much energy into actually doing things as they put into making excuses for not doing things, Everest would be crowded at the top, and construction on Manhattan's streets would finally be finished.

On one level, making excuses is harmless; it's a very normal human thing to do. But in another sense, I see excuses as the single greatest undermining force that keeps people from ever getting started on the *No Opportunity Wasted* lifestyle. Excuses are the "anti-N.O.W.," if you will.

So before we put pencil to paper to begin composing the N.O.W. List for Life, in this chapter we're going to first compile another kind of list—the "Dead Excuses List." Here's the idea: Once you've put an excuse on this list, you have taken it out of circulation. You've declared that excuse to be null and void. Can't use it anymore. Don't even go there.

We're going to include the following 10 great all-purpose excuses on this list. Why these 10? Because they're the ones people most often say to me, and because they really are *good*—they sound perfectly reasonable, rational, and legitimate (which is what makes them so nasty). Here they are.

1. "I don't have the money."
2. "I just don't have the time."
3. "You don't understand, my job *is* my life."
4. "The thing is, my family must always come first."
5. "Look, in my spare time, I just need to relax."
6. "No thanks, not interested in dying right now."
7. "My wife/husband would think I was crazy if I did that!"
8. "Hey, I'm too old for this."
9. "Would love to, but I'm out of shape. And I have that bum knee, too."
10. "To tell you the truth, I just don't think I can do it."

We'll go through each of these excuses one by one as part of the demolition process. Once we've finished with each excuse, write it down on your list. But leave room at the bottom of the list for a few more. Although the top 10 are common excuses that everybody uses, you probably have a few idiosyncratic excuses that are yours and yours alone, and you may want to add those to the list. I'll also cover a handful of "Lame Excuses"—so weak they're almost not worth killing, but we'll do it anyway, and you may want to put those on your list, too.

What should you do with this Dead Excuses List when you're done? I'm tempted to say bury it, but I think it's good to keep it around as a permanent record, kind of like a death certificate. So how about this: When you finish writing the list, carefully place the piece of paper on the floor. Stomp on it with your shoe three or four times, just to make sure the excuses are dead. Then put the list into a drawer somewhere and leave it there. And in the future, if you ever find one of these excuses crossing your lips or your mind again, remember the list and take it out to look at again if necessary. If you find new excuses cropping up over time, add those to the list. (And at any time in this process, if you feel the need to stomp on the list again, that's fine.)

Let's start with the number one excuse people give when I ask them why they don't try to lead more of a N.O.W. life. And that excuse is:

1. "I DON'T HAVE THE MONEY."

This one really drives me crazy. We live in a world where people tend to focus on what they *don't* have instead of what they do. Maybe it's the fault of the media, and in particular advertising, which is often putting out the message that you could lead a better, fuller life if only you had more *stuff* (the latest SUV, the perfect hiking boots, a digital camera). Obviously, all of those things cost money, and so in our heads we come to associate rich and rewarding life experiences with high price tags.

It isn't true, of course. Oftentimes the simplest, most "no-frills" experiences can also be the most rewarding. I learned this early on in my adventure TV career in New Zealand, where production budgets were almost nonexistent and I had to find creative (in other words, dirt cheap) ways to get halfway around the world and have adventures. As we like to say in New Zealand, I produced that show "on the smell of an oily rag" and not much more.

Actually, I learned the lessons of ingenuity even earlier than that—from my parents, who taught me about making the most of limited resources. When I was growing up on the island of Antigua, my mother taught at two different schools on different sides of the island, and one of the schools didn't have typewriters for the students. She would get my sister and me to help her load up our car with typewriters from one school and haul them to the other, so that none of the kids would have to do without. My dad was no less resourceful: His job was to help local farmers find ways to farm more productively, and he set himself up in an old sugarcane factory, surrounded by used equipment and abandoned buildings. One of my most vivid memories is of helping my dad as he turned old railway train carriages into flatbed nurseries for new plants; he could then wheel them around to give them sun or water. To me, it was a great lesson in taking whatever was handy and making the most of it.

This is a theme that has become central to my life and to the *No Opportunity Wasted* philosophy, and one that will be stressed throughout this book. Instead of focusing on the amount of money lacking in your budget, focus on what you *do* have: a willing spirit, an imagination filled with bright ideas, people who care about you and can perhaps help you in some way. These are the things that will enable you to do almost anything. And here's a little secret I've learned: If you *earn* your experiences by utilizing ingenuity, creativity, and a bit of hard work along the way, you will appreciate those experiences much more in the end. Of course, it is possible to, in effect, buy an experience off the shelf. But those aren't the kind of experiences I've ever been interested in; they're too generic, too prepackaged, and too damn *easy*. If everything is bought and paid for, there is no real challenge—and, to my mind, no real adventure. If you go to a foreign country on a chauffeured tour that books you into the cushiest hotels and escorts you to the finest restaurants and takes care of every detail for you, you become insulated from the actual real-life experience of the place you are visiting. After all, if you want to be sheltered, why bother to travel?

On *The Amazing Race*, as we lead the contestants in a race from country to country and from one wild experience to the next, we purposely keep their funds limited because we want to push them to be more resourceful, more imaginative. Similarly, on the new *No Opportunity Wasted* TV series, where in each episode people are challenged to turn a lifelong dream into a reality, we offer a frugal $3,000 budget to everyone, regardless of how complex their dreams might be. Again, the idea is to force people to use *imagination as their currency*.

And it's amazing how people will respond to that challenge. On that modest budget, two young women went halfway around the world, climbed mountains, skydived, paid homage to their late father, and had the adventure of a lifetime. On that same budget, another man booked one of the most elegant concert halls in the country and put his wife onstage so she could live out her dream of performing live; a young boxer set up and launched a wonderful fitness and self-esteem program for inner-city kids; and a postal worker got to live out his dream of being a professional hockey player for a day. How did they do it? I'll tell you more about these individual adventures in chapters ahead, but the general answer is: They worked at it. They searched out the cheapest, most practical ways to do things. They made hard choices and sacrifices, compromising or scaling back on the dream if they had to, sleeping on floors if they had to. They called in favors from people they knew (it seems everybody knows somebody who has an uncle who can help you with your dream—if only you ask). Or in some cases, they turned to strangers for a helping hand and were rarely refused. The effort, the creativity, the hard choices, and the kindness of strangers along the way all become part of the experience, making it richer and more meaningful. Sure, it might be possible in some cases for wealthy people to open their wallets and just "buy" a similar experience. But *No Opportunity Wasted* is about fulfilling dreams, and I would make the case that you can't really "buy" a dream. If you can attain something that easily, then it's not special enough to qualify as a dream.

You may be limited in what you can spend, just like the dreamers on N.O.W. TV; then again, you might not be. But I will work from the assumption that you don't have a lot of money and that you *do* have a lot of heart. Throughout the book, we'll try to offer suggested activities and experiences that are fun, affordable, and practical. Keep in mind that almost every type of experience we'll talk about has different versions: the elaborate version, the scaled-back version, and the versions in between. The book will try to make that clear, but part of your job is to figure out which version of an experience is realistic and attainable for you. Instead of just saying, "I can't afford to travel to that mountain," find another mountain that's closer and cheaper to get to. Remember, the phrase "I don't have the money" is no longer part of your vocabulary—you are banishing it to the Dead Excuses List, as of right now.

2. "I JUST DON'T HAVE THE TIME."

This one runs a close second to the first excuse and is similar in that it also focuses on the *lack* of something. Instead, we should be focused on the time we have and how it is allocated and used. When people say to me, "I don't have time to do that," I try to get them to break down that statement: What exactly do you mean when you say that you "don't have time?" What you're really saying is, "I am not going to make this particular thing a priority in my life," or "I choose not to do this because something else is more important to me."

So in a way, overcoming the time excuse begins with the recognition that living a full, interesting life is "important" enough to make it a priority. If and when you decide that it is (and it's hard to imagine why one would decide otherwise), then you must begin to treat it as a priority by moving it up higher on your overall personal agenda. Dreams tend to be kept far down on the agenda, stuck on the lowly "someday" shelf. Of course, as you begin to move them up, other things (Watching television? Working on the yard? Putting in overtime hours at work?) may have to be moved down. You've got to make some choices if you're going to make time for a N.O.W. life. That may sound difficult, but it's also a good sign when you find yourself having to make tough choices about what to do with your time. It means you're living a full life, with many options available to you.

Living out N.O.W. experiences often doesn't take as much time as people may assume. You don't have to have 3 weeks off in order to do something interesting. In each episode of our television series, people manage to do amazing things that can end up changing their lives—in a span of *72 hours*. That's nothing more than a long weekend. It's the amount of time you might take off when you have a cold, or when attending funeral services. On N.O.W. TV, we will often help "clear the schedule" for our participants for those 3 days, in advance and without their knowledge, because we want to make sure people can't claim "I don't have time to do it now" or "my job can't possibly spare me."

And do you know what I've learned in this process? It's not that hard to clear someone's schedule for a few days. You may think you're indispensable, but sorry, you're not. The office will go on without you. The trains will still

Not Enough Time?
Who Are You Kidding?

Though many people often feel they don't have enough time to do the things they really want to do, they're actually fooling themselves, says time management expert Harold Taylor of Harold Taylor Time Consultants Inc. in Newmarket, Ontario. "We are deceived into thinking we don't have time for other things simply because our time is now being consumed by something else," Taylor says. "It's up to us to choose how we will spend our lives. Displace the boring, routine, nonproductive activities in which you are currently engaged with exciting, vibrant opportunities that will give life greater meaning."

You can also help your cause by cutting down on wasted time at work, Taylor notes. Simply organizing your schedule better and delegating routine activities wherever possible "will free up anywhere from 20 percent to 50 percent of your time," he says. "You could then devote this time to more *vital* activities such as planning and innovating—activities that have bigger payoffs, accomplish significant results, and move you closer to your personal and business goals." Taylor also recommends cutting down on long formal meetings by having "brief stand-up meetings with staff members." And, he adds, beware of perfectionism at work, which can cause you to spend too much time on tasks that aren't worth it.

On the home front, "household activities such as cleaning, maintenance, and gardening can sometimes be outsourced," Taylor says. "Don't spend your own $100-an-hour time doing $20-an-hour jobs. Spend your time on relationships, not upkeep. Use your time on more satisfying pursuits."

run even if you're not in your usual seat at 8:07. In fact, I often encounter bosses who are thrilled to send someone off on an adventure and spouses who are more than happy to pick up the slack and cover for their partners—if they buy into the notion that people deserve a chance to live out their dreams. (Who knows, maybe the spouses are thinking ahead: "Next year, I'll get to chase *my* dream, and it'll be *his/her* turn to cover things.")

If even 3 days seems like a lot to you, then you may need to scale back some adventures. But bear in mind that a N.O.W. moment can happen in . . . literally, a moment. Instead of waiting for blocks of free time, you can look for small openings and fill the little gaps in your schedule. Everybody has a lunch break, and *that* can be an experience. Forget the company cafeteria or the deli down the block: Find an exotic little diner in an offbeat part of town. Or eat your sandwich while hiking through local woods. Find ways to take in new experiences while you're doing something mundane, such as flying around on business trips. It may take some effort and imagination on your part to squeeze N.O.W. moments and experiences into a tight schedule, but think of that as part of the challenge and part of the adventure.

3. "YOU DON'T UNDERSTAND, MY JOB *IS* MY LIFE."

This is related to the time excuse, but it goes beyond time: Workaholics (and I use that term affectionately, because I am sometimes one myself) have a tendency to give not just their time but their *all* to the job. It becomes the reason for being, the place where you invest your hopes and expend your energies, where you rise to personal challenges, test yourself, and so forth. This is not a bad thing: If you have a job that pushes and challenges you this way, you're fortunate (and if you don't have a job like that, we'll get to you in a minute). But the problem with being consumed by your job is that it can burn you out. And make you one-dimensional. Being an architect is interesting, but if you care *only* about architecture, you might not be so fascinating after all.

In the go-go late 1990s, it was okay to be a workaholic; people bragged about the insane hours they spent pursuing business success. But ever since September 11 turned the world upside down, there has been an interesting shift under way. A growing number of people, including very successful business executives, have come to realize that it makes sense to have a life outside the job and that "balance" is a good and worthwhile thing for

How the N.O.W. Life Can Help You in Your Job

Can living adventurously make you better at your work? Clearly, a growing number of companies believe there is a connection between outdoor adventure and enhanced job performance, based on the continued growth of corporate adventure training programs over the past decade. Such programs run the gamut from group wilderness retreats that encourage team-building to rock-climbing courses designed to help executives learn how to "claw their way to the top."

"Adventure teaches you all kinds of skills that are relevant to work," says Nella Barkley, whose human resources consulting company, Crystal-Barkley, advises major corporations on how to help employees become more productive and well-rounded. "It can teach you interpersonal skills which to strive. Now, some of the same people who used to brag about their work are more proud to talk about the fact that they've taken up windsurfing or the violin. And guess what? It doesn't make them any less productive or less dedicated to their jobs. In fact, many are finding that having a life outside the job actually helps make them *better* at their jobs.

Indeed, I have always maintained that if you lead a N.O.W. life outside your job, that lifestyle and attitude almost can't help but spread to every aspect of your life, *including* your job. Once you've tapped into those inner reserves—your own curiosity and inventiveness, your willingness to learn new skills and take chances—you are bound to start applying them to your job. If you can somehow inject the spirit of N.O.W. into your job, you may be able to find ways to bring new excitement to

such as how to lead, how to work as a team, or how to engage with people you don't know, even people who speak a different language. It improves your ability to negotiate tough situations and navigate around obstacles." Indeed, once you've gone through challenging life adventures, tackling everyday business problems may not seem as difficult as before. Some companies are also finding that inspiration—the kind that feeds fresh thinking and big ideas—can be stoked by getting people away from the stifling office environment and exposing them to more-stimulating experiences, whether at a local art exhibit or a faraway nature retreat. When you open yourself up to new experiences, says Barkley, "it tends to rearrange your head and get you thinking in a different way— and that can give you new ideas that might apply to work." It's pretty simple, really: The more you experience in life, the more inner resources you have to draw from when you're at the office.

the workplace. Maybe you can encourage others to help you change the work environment, one small step at a time—setting up a "work outside in the park day" with coworkers, or suggesting a weekly program in which you and coworkers express yourselves by creating art, building something, or putting on a performance of some kind. The possibilities are endless. *Unless . . .* your job is the kind that doesn't allow for possibilities, doesn't make use of your creativity or energy, and doesn't give you any chance to tap into your passion for life. And if *that's* the case, then it may turn out that your N.O.W. List for Life could serve as a career wake-up call and a guideline that can help you change your professional life as well as your personal one. If nothing else, your N.O.W. list should help you figure out what really gets you excited in life—and that can help you identify what you want in a job, too. Perhaps one of the challenges that will end up being added to your List for Life is "I need to go on a journey to find a job that makes me feel alive, one that tests my limits and lets me express myself and reach for the sky."

4. "MY FAMILY MUST ALWAYS COME FIRST."

This is another way of saying, "I'm a grown-up, with grown-up responsibilities; therefore, there's no room for crazy, self-indulgent adventures in my life." I don't buy it. If anything, the fact that you have a family should open you up to more adventures and experiences. If you've got a child, it's all the more reason to be childlike yourself—to explore, to learn new things, to have fun. You have the perfect companions to join you on adventures, because kids can't get enough of them. They learn and grow from them. By the time my daughter, Elle, was 2 years old, she already had frequent-flyer status. I have strapped her on my back as I've biked up and down mountains, and taken her diving with me. And as a result, she's absolutely fearless. She has absorbed the N.O.W. attitude as a child, and I believe it will stay with her throughout her life. On the other hand, if your child sees you leading a cautious, restricted, and mostly joyless life, that gets absorbed, too. Is that the example you wish to set? I think N.O.W. parents are the kind who say to their child, "Sure you can climb that tree—in fact, I'm going to climb it with you."

While there are countless great experiences you can have with your family, don't feel that you're no longer entitled to individual experiences. There are some dreams that are yours alone and should be undertaken that way. It may require you to make a hard choice—taking occasional time for yourself that might have been spent with the kids. But if the experience leaves you more fulfilled, you'll be a better person and, by extension, a better parent. You'll be a little more flexible, a tad more tolerant. If you're stuck in that everyday rut of life, your boredom and frustration levels rise as your patience shrinks. And that doesn't help you be a great parent. Confucius (a very N.O.W. guy, by the way) once said, *"To put the world in order, we must first put the nation in order; to put the nation in order, we must first put the family in order; to put the family in order, we must first cultivate our personal life; we must first set our hearts right."*

5. "IN MY SPARE TIME, I JUST NEED TO RELAX."

The rationale here is that if you live fully and adventurously in your "spare time" (whatever that is), it will drain energy instead of allowing you to rest and recharge. But here's the truth: If you set out on an experience, you will be energized by the experience itself. You may assume that because you have a difficult, exhausting job, you should sprawl on the couch after work and snooze on the beach during your vacations. But lying around does *not* give you more energy. "The more things you do, the more energy you'll have," says Joe Kita of *Men's Health* magazine. That's because leading an active, adventurous life gets adrenaline pumping, releases stimulating endorphins, and strengthens your muscles—all of which helps you feel "charged up" during and even after the experience. "And the more adventurous the activities you do, the longer these aftereffects seem to last," Kita adds.

Another benefit of going on adventures is that it can take your mind off work or other stressful things that may be going on in your life. If you lie on a beach, you may be tempted to think about the problems waiting for you back at the office, but if you're lost in another world—facing your fears or taking on stiff challenges—the office is the last thing on your mind.

6. "NO THANKS, NOT INTERESTED IN DYING RIGHT NOW."

Well, who is? I like living as much as the next guy, and if I really believed there was a good chance a particular experience might kill me, I wouldn't do it myself and certainly wouldn't recommend it to anyone else. If you think an adventurous lifestyle is about risking life and limb every time you venture out, you've got the word adventure confused with the term extreme thrill-seeking (or maybe you've just got it mixed up with the word insanity). Of course there are certain risks inherent in some outdoor experiences, though you may be surprised when you actually look at the statistics and find that so-called "dangerous" activities are not as dangerous as you might think. Moreover, there are ways to ratchet down the risk level on any experience, simply by being smart about it.

What I learned from my own near-death diving experience at age 19 is that you really need to know what you're getting into before you set out to do it. I'm a big proponent of spontaneity in many things, from going skinny-dipping to delving into exotic cultures, but when it comes to activities that have a safety-hazard element involved, I'm a die-hard believer in being prepared. That means educating yourself on what the risks are, getting complete and proper training in advance, and having the recommended safety equipment with you at all times. That may seem like extra work, but think of it as part of the experience. Preparation is the first step on the journey to the actual experience. I talked earlier about *earning* experiences, which will ultimately enhance your feelings of pride and accomplishment; well, preparation is part of the earning process. But it can also be both fun and enlightening. Training courses will begin to challenge you mentally and physically as they show you what lies ahead; they create a sense of camaraderie with other people in the program; and they instill feelings of self-confidence, which you'll carry with you later when you're in the water or on a mountain.

Even with activities that don't require full-fledged training courses, it's always a good idea to do advance research on your own, so that you're fully aware of any risks and safety precautions associated with a given experience. The miracle of Google makes this easier to do than ever before. Don't think of it as homework but rather as part of the fun of learning something you've always wanted to learn. If it doesn't strike you that way as you're doing the research or training, then maybe you need to stop and ask yourself whether you're really interested in this particular experience. If you're not intrigued by the process of becoming a climber, then perhaps you don't really want to be a climber after all. It could be that you

WHAT ARE THE CHANCES?

Sure, there's a certain level of risk in living adventurously, just as there is in stepping outside the door of your house each day (or staying inside, for that matter). To put it all into perspective, here are some relevant numbers.

Chances of getting attacked by a shark: It happens only about 60 times a year worldwide, and that's down 30 percent from a few years ago. You're more likely to be attacked by a dog in your own cozy neighborhood.

Chances of dying from a snakebite: Only one in five snakes are poisonous, and only one in 10 people actually bitten by a snake die. That's 40,000 a year. Food poisoning from shrimp cocktail is more common.

Chances of having a skydiving accident: There are three million jumps a year, and only about 30 people a year die from skydiving.

just want to somehow get to the point of *feeling* like you've climbed a mountain, or perhaps you merely want to see the world from a different, "higher" perspective. If so, there may be other ways to satisfy that urge that are more in sync with your interests. One of the benefits of preparation, training, and research is that it can help clue you in to what you actually like and don't like doing before you've gone too far.

One last thing to be said about risk: Most of the activities we'll talk about in this book do not involve physical risk-taking so much as mental risk-taking. By that, I mean putting yourself in an unfamiliar place, trying something new and strange, and subjecting yourself to the possibility of surprise, which can sometimes bring momentary disorientation

That's a one in 100,000 ratio. You're far more likely to be killed in a commercial airline crash.

Chances that you will slip out of your shoes while bungee jumping: Virtually nonexistent. Only a handful of deaths have been reported worldwide over the past decade, and that encompasses millions of jumps. So the accident ratio is literally one in a million. Contrast this to the one in 6,000 chance that you will die in a car accident in any given year.

Here are few other things that are worth noting.

Chances that you will die at home in your own bed: This happens *a lot.*

Chances that you will die in some kind of a bed: Maybe 90 percent?

Chances that if you stay out of bed, you might live forever: It's just a theory at this point.

Chances that you will die from drinking cobra blood in the jungle: All I can tell you is, I did it and I'm still here.

or embarrassment. These are the kinds of risks we are primarily talking about and, believe me, they will not kill you. They *will* make you feel alive.

7. "MY WIFE/HUSBAND WOULD THINK I WAS CRAZY IF I DID THAT!"

It is not unheard of for a N.O.W. person to be married to a "No Way" person. If this is the case, don't despair. There are two possible solutions, the first one being the more difficult: You can drag your reluctant spouse kicking and screaming into the *No Opportunity Wasted* way of life. (And if you can get past the initial violent reaction, the odds are good that you will be thanked for it in the end.) On the other hand, if you don't wish to push your partner into something, then you can simply . . . go forth without him.

There is nothing wrong with embarking on adventures by yourself. On the other hand, you can also find an "adventure buddy," or a group of them, to accompany you on your journeys. How do you find these kindred souls? Look for groups and associations of people who share your particular interests. Or put the word out at the office or at your health club that you're thinking of undertaking a particular experience. Someone may surface to join you; others will, at least, support you. Let people know what you want to achieve, what your goal is—so you can feed off their encouragement. People tend to rally around someone who's taking on a challenge. (By the way, if certain friends or acquaintances laugh off your dream, bear in mind what Walt Disney once advised: *"Keep away from people who try to belittle your ambitions. Small people always do that."*)

Once you start fully leading the N.O.W. life, you are going to run across more and more people like you—it's inevitable. Out there in the world, there are others whose dreams intersect with yours. But you may never know about these people until you act on the dream. A friend of mine really wanted to take up bike racing, and her husband just wasn't into it; she joined a club of female cyclists, and they've inspired her to reach a very high level. When you're surrounded by people who are enthusiasts about something, you get pulled along by the momentum.

On *The Amazing Race*, I often saw the benefits of partnerships when going on an adventure. One person might take the lead in a particular challenge, and the other would do so on the next. Partners tend to support and push each other—and that can be enough to get you to the other side of a difficult hurdle. This is why it's great to have an "adventure buddy"—and that person might happen to be an old pal, a new acquaintance, a coworker, a sibling, or someone other than your spouse. This shouldn't be a problem, as long as you make it clear to your spouse that this experience is important to you and that you're willing to return the favor and offer support as soon as she decides to pursue her own dream. Heck, your spouse could probably use a break from you every once in a while. And you'll have more to talk about when you get back.

8. "I'M TOO OLD FOR THIS."

If you believe this, then it's your attitude that is old, and you need to look around at what's happening in the world. People are living longer, fuller lives. Retirees are participating in adventure travel as never before. There are more diverse activities geared to seniors than ever before, more accessible challenges. On my own experiences with *The Amazing Race*, I've seen grandmothers bungee jump—and love it! I've seen older people outperform younger people time and time again. Here are some other things I've observed about older people on adventures or experiences: They often surprise themselves with how young they are. And they tend to take even more pride and satisfaction in their accomplishments, because they know they've overcome more obstacles than a younger person doing the same thing. Among the people you'll meet in this book are an 89-year-old man who water-skis and snowboards (chapter 7), as well as a woman in her seventies who is a triathlon champion (chapter 5), and others. What they all have in common is a spirit that refuses to grow old.

9. "I'M TOO OUT OF SHAPE."

This excuse is sometimes accompanied by a mention of the "bum knee," the "bad back," or the shoulder that was operated on 6 years ago. It is rooted in the assumption that you must be in top shape before you can begin a more active life. But think about it: This logic is completely backward, of course. Only by leading a more active life will you ever become more fit. And if you wait around for the time when your back is feeling perfect or your bod is totally buff, that day may never arrive. I hate to see people create a two-step process for themselves, in which they must first get in shape at the gym and *then* they'll try all those other fun things they dream of doing. Because they may never get beyond that first stage, especially if they view it as a chore.

There's no reason to get caught up in worrying about fitness in advance, because depending on what goes on your List for Life, fitness may not be a big issue anyway. Many of the dreams you end up pursuing may be more of a mental challenge than a physical one. And if you do opt to take on more physical challenges, there are ways to build up to them with baby steps, or "milestones," which we'll discuss throughout the book.

Finally, keep this in mind: Whatever your physical imperfections or impediments might be, there is somebody out there who is dealing with much greater physical hardship and is still living the N.O.W. life. In my own travels, I've come to know many such inspirational people. Some years ago, I met a woman who took up running to try to strengthen the clubbed feet she was born with. She trained and trained as her feet bled, and ended up breaking a track record for 5000 meters. More recently, I've gotten to know Jesse

Billauer (who is featured in chapter 5), a paralyzed surfer who refuses to give up riding the waves. There are countless other examples, and perhaps people in your own life, who demonstrate that you do not have to be a perfect physical specimen to achieve amazing things.

10. "I JUST DON'T THINK I CAN DO IT."

In some ways, I respect this excuse the most because at least it's honest. It cuts to the core of what really stops so many of us from taking risks, trying something new, accepting challenges—and that is *fear of failure*. It is one of the biggest, most pernicious fears out there, and I'll talk more about it in the next chapter, Face Your Fear. But for now, let me just make a couple of brief points about this. First and foremost: *You cannot fail at the N.O.W. lifestyle.* It is not results-based but rather experience-based. Just by getting out there and trying something, you've succeeded in terms of experiencing something you never would've known otherwise. The other point to make here is that a lot of dreams or goals tend to seem impossible before you've started. They begin to seem a little more possible as soon as you take the first step, which this book will help you do. With each successive step you take after that, the dream becomes more and more real. As Francis of Assisi said, *"Start by doing what's necessary, then what's possible, and suddenly you are doing the impossible."*

AND LAST, I GIVE YOU . . .
THE LAME EXCUSES

"I can't think of anything particularly interesting that I really want to do." Okay, this sounds truly pathetic, but it's actually quite common. And the reason is, you haven't taken the time or effort to really think about this. Interesting, meaningful ideas won't come to you unless you put a bit of effort into the thought process. I like this little musing from the author James Truslow Adams: *"Perhaps it would be a good idea, fantastic as it sounds, to muffle every telephone, stop every motor, and halt all activity for an hour some day, to give people a chance to ponder for a few minutes on what it is all about, why they are living and what they really want."* Well, maybe you can't stop the world, but you can close yourself off from it for an hour: just you, your imagination, your pen, and your list . . . for a full hour. You might be surprised at the results.

"My dog will miss me while I'm away." Fine. Take him along for the ride. I went scuba diving with a dog once. You heard me right: The pooch had his own little diving helmet and air tank, made by his owner, Dwayne Folsom. (Dwayne had no choice in the matter: Whenever he tried to go scuba diving, the dog would get mad at being left alone on the boat.) There are lots of other things you can do with your pet, too; a growing number of adventure travel outfitters are offering trips for people and their pets. Colorado Canines in Boulder offers Colorado Adventure Trips where you can go river rafting with your dog (wouldn't recommend this with the cat, however). You can also go camping with your dog at Camp Dogwood, just north of Chicago.

"Why bother to go on an adventure when I can just watch one on TV?" As someone who is in the midst of the reality television phenomenon, permit me to now bite the hand that feeds me by saying the following: Watching "reality" is a poor substitute for experiencing it. Too many people are starting to believe that living vicariously is the same as living imaginatively. We watch others pursue that dream job with Donald Trump, or sing their hearts out on *American Idol*, or test their survival skills on an island. And the whole time, we're stuck in a chair. I believe that one reason *Survivor*, *The Amazing Race*, and other shows struck a nerve is that they tapped into a longing deep within us. As modern-day life has become safer and more predictable, we still hunger to be challenged and tested, to make use of our survival skills and our frontier spirit. We still want to experience that in some way—and so we now watch a television show where people are put on an island, stripped of modern-day conveniences and protections, and pushed to the limit. This can be fun to observe, without a doubt. But there's a time for watching and a time for doing. Think of it this way: *Your life is the ultimate reality show.* And you better get out of that chair and start doing your part—because one of these days, you're going to get voted off the island.

"This all sounds great . . . but it's just not *me*." I hate this excuse because it makes it sound as if people have no control over their own identities. It's as if they feel they have to live up to their own self-image—even though they may not like that image. And heaven forbid, if they've never done offbeat, interesting, slightly wild things in the past and suddenly start now . . . it might seem *out of character*. What will other people think? You can't just become a free spirit overnight, can you? Sure you can. I have seen librarians climb mountains. I have seen a middle-aged nun win an Ironman competition. I have seen a nice Orthodox Jewish boy who lived with his mother become a "gangsta" hip-hop rapper (see chapter 8). All of these people

(continued)

(continued)

THE LAME EXCUSES

decided to move beyond the narrow identities that seemingly defined them—and in doing so, they made themselves a little harder to pigeonhole and a little more interesting to the people around them. And if their newfound N.O.W. spirit seemed surprising to others at first, it soon came to be accepted (even by the mother of the nice-Jewish-boy-turned rapper).

"It's not that I'm scared, but . . ." This is a really lame excuse because it usually means you are scared and don't want to say it. It's okay to be scared; we all are. The problem comes when you deny it instead of facing it. I believe that even though there are endless variations on excuses, many of them are rooted in some form of fear—fear of failure, of danger, of the unknown, or of embarrassment. The excuses rise to the surface, but the fear is what's underneath, feeding those excuses.

And that is why, as we set out to begin making the *No Opportunity Wasted* List for Life, the first item on it—the first thing you will choose to do as you begin this lifestyle—will be to *face your fear*.

3

FACE YOUR FEAR

"You gain strength, courage, and confidence by every experience in which you really stop to look fear in the face. You must do the thing you think you cannot do."

—ELEANOR ROOSEVELT

ON A RECENT WARM sunny day in the Bahamas, Shane Platt found himself floating along in a crystal-clear blue ocean, accompanied by about 50 other swimmers. But Shane was having trouble enjoying the moment—perhaps because the other swimmers circling around him all happened to be sharks.

This would be enough to make anyone uneasy, but it was even worse for Shane because he suffered from *selachophobia*—a persistent and acute fear of sharks. It's normal to be wary of anything that can bite you in half, but Shane's fear ran especially deep, having taken hold of him when he was a child. He thinks it all started when he watched the film *Jaws*. Yes, it was only a movie, and no, he'd never encountered an actual shark in his life. But the fear was nevertheless real and palpable, and it stayed with him through adulthood, causing nightmares. Moreover, it had a profound effect on his life, because Shane, wouldn't you know it, had a passion for underwater diving.

Shane mastered his scuba-diving skills in the freshwater (and blessedly shark-free) Great Lakes of his home state, Michigan. But diving in the ocean was a different kettle of fish. During his 5 years in the Navy, Shane steadfastly refused to submerge himself in ocean waters. And in the years since, he'd turned down numerous offers from fellow divers to join them in exploring ocean shipwrecks around the world. Shane hated to say no to these offers; he knew he was closing himself off from a world of rich experiences. On one occasion, he forced himself to say yes and went to Florida to dive an ocean wreck. He never saw a shark but was so petrified of the *possibility* of seeing one that he almost passed out; afterward, his mind blanked out the whole experience. For a long while thereafter, Shane was prepared to admit defeat. It seemed the sharks had won the battle going on in his mind without ever so much as making an appearance in his actual life.

One day in late 2003, Shane wrote a letter to me at the *No Opportunity Wasted* TV series, explaining that he wanted to finally face this fear that was restricting his freedom. He suggested that perhaps, with a little help and encouragement from N.O.W., he could force himself to go on a professionally supervised shark dive. His trepidation came through even in this letter: "While I am not super-excited to start off with a shark dive," he wrote, "perhaps we could work up to it by doing a nice friendly dolphin dive (do dolphins have teeth?)." What also came through was how much this meant to Shane, on more than one level. He talked about wanting to "see the beauty of the ocean that my dive buddies keep telling me about, everything from the amazing coral to the exotic little fish." He talked about the need to prove something to his friends and his family, who, he said, "would never believe that I would do such a feat." And finally he added: "I know that if I got this opportunity, I would become both a better person and a better diver for it."

How could I resist such a heartfelt request from a fellow in need? And on top of that, how could I resist a trip to the Bahamas and a chance to go mess around with some man-eating creatures? In early 2004, I met up with Shane and his best friend, Ron, and we went to see Stuart Cove, a professional shark wrangler in the Bahamas who arranges and supervises shark dives. Stuart had a three-step plan in mind for Shane. First, we would go to a shark aquarium, where Shane could face the object of his anxieties in safety from behind a glass partition. In the second step, Shane would feed sharks while standing on land; he could still turn tail and run if necessary. Last, Shane would dive into the water with the sharks, at which point there would be no escape.

Stuart Cove and I accompanied Shane on the first leg of the journey to face his fear. At the aquarium, we stood watching from behind the glass as a black-tipped beauty swam up to us. Shane's eyes widened, and he muttered, "Look at the size of him—must be five feet long!" Then he glanced at Stuart, who nodded and shared some information he thought Shane should know.

"The sharks you are going to be diving with," he said, "are about twice that size."

If Shane was beginning to get a tad nervous in the aquarium, his fear escalated as we moved to the second of his three tasks. We traveled by boat to a small lagoon for an encounter with sharks in the wild. We stood in shallow water as a couple of Cove's wranglers lured some sharks in close to the shore, using bait attached to ropes. After a while, Shane reluctantly agreed to take hold of one of the ropes. He stood waiting, his body stiff and tight. He saw the dorsal fin approach and felt a little tug on his line. Then, as the shark snatched the bait, Shane felt the incredible

(continued on page 54)

On the Next *Oprah:* Two People at the End of Their Ropes!

I've never been afraid of heights myself. But after briefly seeing things from the perspective of an acrophobe named Mitu Banerjee, I gained a new appreciation of the challenges faced by her and others like her. I came to know Mitu because I received a call, about a year ago, from *The Oprah Winfrey Show.* In a segment on people facing fears, the show's producers wanted to feature Mitu. And no wonder: A dynamic, successful woman, Mitu seemed to have just one thing holding her back. Her fear of heights kept her from flying in airplanes with her husband and leading the full life she deserved. My assignment was to help Mitu "rise above" this problem while Oprah's viewers watched.

The plan was to bring Mitu up onto the tallest bridge in the United States, the New River Gorge Bridge, which is located in West Virginia, and have her rappel 250 feet down to the ground below. I decided to approach this in steps, or "milestones," that she could get past one at a time. The first step was to try to prepare her, mentally, for the challenge. We sat down and talked about this fear; it had plagued her since she was a child and kept her from even climbing a ladder. We talked about the irrationality of it and about real versus imagined risks. We also talked about why it was so important for her to overcome this fear, and the reasons she felt, deep inside, that it was worth confronting. By the end of the conversation, we were feeling quite calm and rational about the whole thing—but, of course, it's easy to be rational when you're still on the ground.

The next step was to take Mitu to the bridge but not to the top. I felt we should start at the ground below, looking up at the bridge. Obviously, it's not as scary looking up as looking down. But in addition, this gave her a chance to actually stand on the solid ground that would later be her destination point as we rappelled down. I wanted her to know this was a safe, comfortable place—she wasn't going to be dropping down into the unknown. Next, we went up onto the bridge. There was a walkway that extended out on girders; this was to be our launching point. But just to get onto that walkway, we had to first climb a ladder. I knew this would be really tough for Mitu, so I set up a harness to support her as she climbed the steps. Once we were out on the walkway, we had to walk on a beam; again, we did it in stages—take a couple of steps, then stop and regroup. "See how you feel after each step," I said to her. "If you feel good, we'll keep going. If not, we can always go back." She kept looking into my eyes, as I'd suggested. I could tell she was unnerved by the sound of cars swooshing by on the bridge just above. A bit of outside perspective can help at times like this, so I reminded her, "Hey, you're not the only one up here who wants to live through this, you know. I don't plan on letting *either* of us fall."

When it was time to rappel, I reminded Mitu that she was secured by not just one but two separate cables, for extra security. Still, it's always hard to force your feet to leave the solid surface and push off into the air, with only a rope to keep you from falling. I demonstrated first for her, rappelling off the bridge on my rope; as I dangled just beneath her, I told her to keep looking at me as she pushed off herself. Once she made that little jump, the hardest part was over, though she didn't realize it yet. As we simultaneously lowered

(continued)

(continued)

TWO PEOPLE AT THE END OF THEIR ROPES!

ourselves, our eyes were still locked together. "Don't look away until you're ready," I told her. I think because I was staring into her eyes so intensely, I suddenly started to *feel her fear*—a strange experience for someone who'd done so many skydives and bungee jumps. It made me appreciate the tremendous courage she was displaying. When we were about halfway down, her eyes began to unlock from mine and peek around. "Don't look down," I said. But then she surprised me.

"No, no," she said softly, "I think it's okay. I think I can look now." And she did. She could see that familiar ground, getting closer with each moment. After that, she just got stronger and stronger. By the time we touched down, she was elated.

Building on her newfound confidence, Mitu recently flew in a small plane for the first time. "I've been seeing things in a different light ever since I climbed down from that bridge," she says now. "It surprised me how good it felt to face that fear. Now I feel like I want to take more chances." So what new heights does she plan to scale? "Maybe I'll try parasailing. I think I'm going to put that on my list." (For Mitu's list, see chapter 11.)

power of a 200-pound hungry beast; the force yanked and almost pulled him into the water. The wranglers, who understood this power so well, just laughed, but as I looked at Shane's face, he seemed to be in a mild state of shock. I'm sure he was already thinking about what was to come the next day, when there would be no glass walls or long ropes, and when his limbs would dangle in the water like that bait on the end of the line.

As we rested up and waited for the big dive, it was clear to me that Shane was becoming increasingly agitated. His pal Ron tried to console him and then told me, "I don't know if he's going to be able to go through with it. Shane underrates himself." Ron talked with me about a recent experience in which Shane had tried to take a cave-diving course. He quit about halfway through, just couldn't go any deeper into the hole and had to tell the instructor to stop the dive. "Shane was very hard on himself afterward," Ron said. "He has a lot of inner turmoil about what he can and can't do. This is a real mountain he has to get over. If he can do it, I think it would open up a whole new world for him."

Later on, I found Shane alone on the beach, just a few hours before he would take the big dive. We talked about everything *but* sharks, it seemed: about his feelings of responsibility to his kids and his worries about his job, about his parents and how they had failed to take risks in their own lives and eventually regretted it. "After my mother died," Shane told me, "my father said to me, 'Remember, you have to live each day as if it's your last!'" Clearly, Shane had taken his father's words to heart; it's what brought him to this point. But now he seemed on the verge of slipping back. "I'm not a confident man," he confessed to me, his eyes averted. We both understood, at this point, that this experience was about far more than overcoming one narrow and specific fear. For Shane, it had come to be about whether he was going to succeed or fail at living his life. He put his head down and his shoulders jerked; I realized he was crying. "I don't think I can do it," he said, so quietly that it seemed he was talking only to himself.

THE DEPTH OF FEELING Shane revealed in that conversation on the beach was something of a surprise to me. But at the same time it wasn't, because it confirmed what I have always believed about fears: There is more to them than you think. They run deeper and broader than you might suspect. And their impact on your life can be more pervasive than you could ever imagine. That's why I believe that if you are about to set out on a fuller, more adventurous life, a good place to start is that dark little corner where your fear lives. Facing that fear should be at the top of your List for Life. Because if you don't deal with this issue up front, it may very well impinge on the rest of your list.

It may seem on the surface that Shane's fear of sharks—or, in your own case, perhaps a fear of heights or public speaking or tight spaces—is merely a limited, isolated problem that doesn't have all that much impact on life in general. And so the solution, for some, is simply to dodge that particular fear by avoiding certain specific activities and experiences: "Well, I'll just stay away from crowds, or mountains, and I'll be fine." When you do this, what you're saying, in effect, is: "I'm going to let an irrational fear conquer my better judgment, my spirit, and my will. But only in this one instance."

It doesn't work that way, however. If you give in and admit defeat by one fear, you're inviting others to creep in and conquer you, as well. You've made yourself vulnerable by accepting, in your own mind, that you're not strong enough to beat fear when it rises up against you. And it *will* rise up against you, in more ways than one. In Shane's case, the fear of sharks that had plagued him previously was soon followed by the fear of caves, causing him to suffer another emotional defeat. That setback no doubt weakened him a little bit more, setting him up for the next one—which might not involve sharks or caves but confronting a murky problem at work or in his personal life. One little fear becomes two, three, five. Pretty soon you're saying, "Well, as long as I make sure I avoid heights *and* deep water *and* crowds *and* bumblebees *and* conflict with other humans, I'll be fine!" Of course, living in this restricted manner requires that you gradually close more and more doors in life, for fear of what's on the other side. And this is the absolute antithesis of the N.O.W. lifestyle, which is about continually *opening* as many new doors as possible.

THE ROOT OF THE PROBLEM

All of us have fears, whether we've acknowledged their existence or not. Sometimes we're painfully aware of a particular fear and may even discuss it openly with others, as Shane did with his fear of sharks. Other times, the fear is more hidden. It's there, deep inside, but we may not want to acknowledge it to others or even to ourselves. Susan Jeffers, Ph.D., an expert on fear and the author of the book *Feel the Fear and Do It Anyway*, says that one sign of hidden fears is the tendency to blame others for your own shortcomings. "Whenever we blame anyone for our unhappiness or our inability to act, it's a clue that we are too frightened to take responsibility for our own lives," Dr. Jeffers says.

Where do your fears originate? A psychiatrist could probably trace the source of some of your own particular phobias, though it might require a couple of years of therapy. My own general unscientific theory, offered here quick and cheap, is that we come into the world bright-eyed and without fear, and then gradually begin to accumulate little fears as part of our life experience. Many fears may come from the lessons we learned (or failed to learn) as kids, from something we experienced firsthand or perhaps just observed. In a particular situation, if we notice hesitation or caution on the part of our parents or an older brother, we internalize that and say, "Well, I guess this is something that should scare *me*, too." In any case, my own

Fears That Could Get in the Way of a N.O.W. Life

If you have any of these, you might want to confront them before you go any further.

Acrophobia: fear of heights

Agrizoophobia: fear of wild animals

Ancraophobia: fear of wind

Anthrophobia: fear of humans, public speaking

Apeirophobia: fear of infinity

Asthenophobia: fear of fainting

Atelophobia: fear of imperfection

Atychiphobia: fear of failure

Automysophobia: fear of being dirty

Bathophobia: fear of stairs or steep slopes

Blennophobia: fear of slime

Catagelophobia: fear of being ridiculed

Catapedaphobia: fear of jumping

Chorophobia: fear of dancing

Cremnophobia: fear of precipices

Cyclophobia: fear of bicycles

Dendrophobia: fear of trees

Eleutherophobia: fear of freedom

feeling is that analyzing the original, long-forgotten source of the fear may not be nearly as important as what you choose to do about it, *right now*.

What's interesting about fear is that it is often irrational. If you analyze it and break it down, it may make little sense—but that doesn't make

Geliophobia: fear of laughter

Gymnophobia: fear of nudity

Herpetophobia: fear of reptiles

Ideophobia: fear of ideas

Levophobia: fear of things to the left side of the body

Metathesiophobia: fear of changes

Metrophobia: fear of poetry

Mnemophobia: fear of memories

Neophobia: fear of anything new, reluctance to consume new food

Oneirophobia: fear of dreams

Optophobia: fear of opening one's eyes

Panophobia: fear of everything

Scopophobia: fear of being seen

Siderophobia: fear of stars

Sophophobia: fear of learning

Soteriophobia: fear of dependence on others

Tachophobia: fear of speed

Teleophobia: fear of definite plans

Testophobia: fear of taking tests

Uranophobia: fear of heaven

Xylophobia: fear of forests

Zemmiphobia: fear of the great mole rat

the fear any less compelling. Some fears seem to be based on a distorted or exaggerated sense of oneself, as in "Everybody's going to be watching me," or "Sure the pull-cord on the parachute works for everybody else, but I'm different," or "That dog is going to pick me of all people to bite." When people have self-centered fears like these, the temptation is to say, "Get over yourself—you're not that special!" But, of course, that's not likely to work because rational arguments, in and of themselves, won't overcome an irrational fear.

Statistics and hard data probably won't work either. For example, you may instinctively feel that anything involving heights—mountain climbing, paragliding, bungee jumping, or even flying in airplanes—is inherently dangerous, even though there may be hard evidence and facts to prove that's not the case. Many people are terrified at just the *thought* of doing something like bungee jumping, believing deep down that something awful is bound to happen to them if they try it. Now, if you had this fear, I could explain to you that there are bungee-jump operations that have been in business for a decade or more, encompassing millions of jumps, with not one single fatality; in other words, you would be as safe doing this as driving your car around the block. After showing you reams of reassuring statistics, I could present you with one testimonial after another about the safety of this activity. But chances are, your fear would persist, because it is irrational.

SHIFTING THE BALANCE OF POWER

So how do you overcome something that is paralyzing, that is tangled up deep within you, and that is impervious to logic or reason? In a word: experience. Each time you have a direct encounter with a long-held fear, you stand to gain a little more power over that fear—*if* you can get through the experience without giving up or retreating (if you quit halfway through, the fear may actually get worse). From the first time you make it through one of these experiences, the balance of power starts to shift from the *fear being in charge* of you to *you being in charge* of the fear. You may not eliminate that fear completely; there may always be traces of it that linger and surface from time to time. But when that happens, you will know, from experience, that your mind is more powerful than the fear. That knowledge and confidence will enable you to live with the fear and do all the N.O.W. things you want to do, in spite of it.

It sounds easy, but of course it isn't. Forcing yourself to experience something that terrifies you—in other words, facing your fear—is difficult because you're bound to experience uncomfortable and uncertain moments in the process, and there's no guarantee you won't succumb to the fear along the way. You may reach the point, as Shane did on the beach just before his shark dive, when you are teetering on the edge of going forward or retreating. And if you do end up retreating, you will have suffered another emotionally devastating setback.

The idea is to find ways to deal with the discomfort and uncertainty so that you can decrease your chances of giving in to the fear. And there are concrete steps you can take to help ensure that this happens.

The first step is to *get to know your fears:* Identify what they are (if you don't already know), try to acknowledge their existence without being ashamed of them, and start learning more about them. I mentioned earlier that rational arguments *in and of themselves* can't overcome an irrational fear; only experience will do that. But as you go forth and face a fear, knowledge is a useful tool to have in your back pocket. When the going gets tough and you need to reassure yourself, you can do so with confidence that the person talking you through the experience knows what she is talking about.

Once you've thought about your fear, learned more about it, and

KNOW YOUR FEAR

As you begin to prepare a List for Life, it's important to first think about the various fears that may have kept you from doing new and exciting things in the past. I tend to view fear as an adversary, often an old one that has been stirring up trouble for a long time. And if you're going to try to take on that adversary, it's a good idea to know what you're up against. Start by identifying one or more major fears that have emerged repeatedly in your life. Ask yourself the following questions, just to get on more familiar terms with your nemesis or nemeses.

- What is your earliest memory of having this fear?
- What kind of physical reactions do you have to this fear?
- What are some things this fear keeps you from doing?
- How might your life change if you were able to overcome this fear?

Next, do some homework. Immerse yourself in this particular fear. If you're afraid of snakes, learn more about them. Where do they hide, what do they eat, what makes them mad, which types are actually poisonous, what do you do if you are bitten, what are the actual statistics on snakebite fatalities, what are the common myths? Read up on the subject, and better still, talk to people who know about snakes. Go look at some in a safe setting, such as a snake conservatory, before you venture out into the jungle.

decided you're ready to face it, it's time to begin thinking of an experience that will allow you to face it in a rich, meaningful, and memorable way. We're thinking *big* here. The possibilities are wide-open, but ideally the choice you decide on should combine your fear with something positive, something you *really* want to do. When I decided to face my fear of claustrophobia, I tried to think of an experience that would be confining yet at the same time inspiring and uplifting. I'd heard about an underwater cave, located beneath the Yucatán jungle, that ran 10 miles long with a small opening at each end—the longest underwater cave known to man. Not many people have gone into this cave, but those who have describe its inner beauty as being almost surreal and otherworldly: white cave walls, incredible stalactites resembling works of art, and the awesome roots of the jungle trees dangling down from the land above and floating in the water. I knew that if I could get myself to venture into that cave, my feelings of anxiousness would be counterbalanced by a sense of joy and wonder. It seemed an irresistible adventure. So I wrote it down on my list.

THE IMPORTANCE OF "RAMPING UP"

The experience that you choose to write on your list should be no less exciting to you. If one doesn't immediately spring to mind, that's understandable. You may have to spend time focusing in on this to come up with the ideal possibility, and I'll ask you to do that when we finish with this chapter. In the meantime, we'll move ahead to the next step on the road to facing your fear. Let's say you've identified and learned more about your fear, *and* you've dreamed up an amazing way to face it. At this point, you may be tempted to jump right into the experience, but I've found that it's often wiser to "ramp up" to the big challenge by first tackling smaller challenges that involve the same fear.

Consider the way Shane Platt approached his shark dive. First, he came face-to-face with the sharks in the aquarium; next, he stood in the water and fed them (and by the way, if you're thinking of feeding sharks yourself, I've got a few firsthand tips for you in the box). For Shane, getting through these two "milestones" would prove helpful later on, when it came time to actually dive with the sharks. These safe encounters lessened some of the mystery of the unknown, which tends to exacerbate fears.

How to Hand-Feed a Shark

• First of all, don't use your hand. If a shark takes food out of your hand, the hand then becomes associated with food. That's a bad association.

• Use the proper utensils. A metal skewer with grouper on the end works well. If you want a little more distance, use a rope with grouper on it.

• Try not to get distracted. Once when I was feeding a shark for a morning TV program, I was simultaneously serenaded live by the singer Gladys Knight. It almost caused me to stop paying attention to the shark. Almost.

• If you're right-handed, hold the skewer in your left hand. Just in case.

• Bring a chaperone on your dinner date. In other words, don't feed a shark (or dive with one) unless it's under the supervision of a licensed shark expert.

• Don't expect the shark to be grateful. Sharks aren't like dolphins. In fact, you can get more intimate with a whale than with a shark. (Not that you'd *want* intimacy with a shark.)

In the case of my own cave-diving experience, I prepared by first doing some research on underwater caves, reading descriptions and looking at photos to try to take away some of the mystery of what I'd encounter once I got in there. Something else I did was to give myself little tests to see if I could get my body to relax while enclosed in confining dark places, including the inside of a closet (which might not seem scary to you, but trust me, it's no picnic for someone who's claustrophobic). What really helped, however, was taking myself deep inside a dry cave before I went into the underwater cave. This particular spot (known as the Rat's Nest Cave) was incredibly confining—at one point, I had to slide on my back between two slabs of rock that were so close together, I couldn't even raise my arms. This experience challenged me to confront my claustrophobia without having the added challenge of being underwater and on an air tank. Once I got through that dry-cave experience, I felt much more confident in going into the underwater cave. When I did it, I still had to battle my own fears, but there was never any question of who would win the battle (in fact, the struggle was over within minutes of my going down into that watery hole; from that point on, the experience was pure pleasure and probably one of the top five N.O.W. moments of my entire life).

WINNING THE MIND GAME

I want to be candid here: Preparing and taking these kinds of "baby steps" in advance will help when it's time to face the larger, more frightening experience. *But . . .* that experience still won't be easy, and shouldn't be. There will come that moment when the fear rises up and you wonder: *Am I going to be able to get through this?* Everyone has their own methods of "coming to grips" in this moment of truth, but through the years, I've found a few that are particularly reliable and useful. In the end, much of it comes down to the mind game that you play with yourself and whether or not *you* are running it. It's usually not the physical manifestations of fear (that is, "the jitters") that will do you in; it's the thoughts in your head, running wild and trying to drag you with them. Keeping those thoughts under control, slowing them down, guiding them in the right direction—that's the trick, and some people are better than others at exerting and maintaining this kind of control. But I believe (and know from my own experience) that you can improve in this area by continually testing yourself. Your self-control, your will, your

THE BIGGEST FEAR OF ALL

It's not sharks, or snakes, or heights. The *fear of failure* is number one. And to attack this fear, you must start by asking yourself a simple question: *How do I define failure?* If you tend to measure success or failure in absolute "all-or-nothing" terms, that may be a big part of the problem. Pursuing big ambitious dreams and N.O.W. moments requires that you be more flexible in the way you define success. For example, if you set out on a particular journey and get diverted onto another path because of unforeseen circumstances, that's not a failure—it's simply a different experience (and maybe a better one). One thing I recommend to people as they're planning future experiences is to aim very high, shooting for the ideal—while understanding in advance that it probably won't work out exactly as planned. In other words, be an extreme optimist with a touch of the realist. With this mind-set, you're more psychologically prepared to scale back and compromise if necessary.

ability to guide your own thoughts—these are muscles that grow stronger as you use and stretch them.

And these are strengths that can serve you well in many situations, beyond just scary adventures. Taking on our *biggest* fear is a great way to put our other fears into perspective. If someone who is deathly afraid of heights proves he can get past something as scary as that, then less terrifying fears—of changing jobs, or starting a new business—tend to seem easy to conquer by comparison. The sense of achievement and confidence that comes from getting the better of your fears, whether in the water or on a mountain or in a strange land, tends to spill over into the more "everyday" aspects of your life.

The realist in you will recognize that these compromises are not failures but just practical responses to real-life situations. Meanwhile, the optimist in you will be looking for silver linings all along the way.

In the end, just taking part in a larger-than-life experience—however it may turn out—can be viewed as a success. On *The Amazing Race*, people are eliminated each week, meaning that technically they've "lost" or "failed." But I have yet to see anyone come away from the experience with any feelings of regret or failure. Virtually every one of those eliminated contestants has ended up saying it was one of the best things they'd ever done in life.

If you pursue an experience and fall prey to Murphy's Law, with everything going wrong (it's happened to me more times than I can count), the key is to maintain flexibility and a sense of humor. In a funny way, mishaps can sometimes make an adventure more memorable and provide fodder for good stories. Moreover, the mistakes you make are part of the experience and help show you how to get it right the next time.

Tips on Coming to Grips

When you feel fear rising up in you, how do you stay in control?

Talk to yourself. This has the dual benefit of releasing tension and exposing you to a familiar voice of reason. I talk to myself all the time in sticky situations, saying all the obvious things like, "Hang in there," "You can do this," "Focus on the next step," as well as the old favorite, "Phil, you've really done it to yourself this time." Remind yourself that you've done your homework and taken the necessary precautions (assuming you have; if you haven't, lie to yourself). To quote the Greek philosopher Epictetus: *"What ought one to say then as each hardship comes? I was practicing for this, I was training for this."*

Lean on somebody. If you can face your fear with a buddy, it helps tremendously. Your partner can talk you through, or just listen as you talk yourself through. And if your partner gets spooked? It gives *you* an opportunity to play the hero—taking your mind off your own fear.

Don't worry about "the jitters." Hemingway said, *"Courage is grace under pressure"*—all well and good if you're the Hemingway type. Normal folks are apt to respond to extreme pressure by getting a little shaky in the hands and wobbly in the knees. It just means that your warning systems are functioning properly and useful adrenaline is flowing. The plus side of the jitters is that they tend to make you more alert and focused on

ALL OF WHICH I ENDEAVORED to explain to Shane Platt on that lonely beach before the dive. "Imagine how your kids will feel knowing that you've faced this challenge," I said. "There are going to be things they'll face in their lives that will scare them—and if they know you did this, it's an example that can give them strength." I once again the task at hand. Deep breaths can help ensure that the jitters don't get out of control, as can stretching and "shaking out" nervous arms and legs.

Reinterpret the signal. Susan Jeffers, Ph.D., notes that people often instinctively interpret the sensation of fear as a red-light signal to retreat, rather than as a green light to move ahead. By continually "pushing through" that fear signal instead of going back, you can gradually condition yourself to have more of a "go" response when you feel fear. In the end, the fear sensation is what you make of it: Try welcoming that feeling, embracing it, and riding on the wave of energy it brings. You're not scared, you're "juiced up!"

Take it one leg at a time. When undertaking a scary task, divide it into stages, pit stops, or "escape hatches" along the way. When I was going into the underwater cave, I figured out where the quarter-point was and then the halfway point. I told myself, "I can always turn back before the halfway mark, and after that I'm on my way to being done." At each quarter-point, I stopped and regrouped, just trying to get to the next destination point. This approach can work with all kinds of frightening activities: A friend who was afraid of public speaking told me that he used to break up his speeches into "stopping points" (he'd stop for questions or show a video clip) so he could gather himself. He didn't have to think in terms of making it through the whole speech, only to the next break point.

mentioned his cautious parents. "You don't want to continue that pattern, Shane. Now, right here, you have an opportunity to break from it."

And he did. He lowered himself into that water with four dozen sharks, a tremendous act of courage on his part. He had a little help and some insurance, and there's nothing wrong with that. A chain-mail suit covered him from head to toe. Stuart Cove was watching from the boat. Ron was in the water, close by. And I was in that water, too, looking Shane in the eye, as I'd promised I would—he said he didn't want to look at the sharks. I took a peek and saw them swirling and circling directly beneath us. Then the feeding frenzy began—but we weren't what they chose from the menu, because sharks would rather just eat fish, particu-

FACE YOUR FEAR: POSSIBILITIES

It's time to fill in the first item on your list, in the Face Your Fear category (write it in pencil; you may come up with a better idea as you keep thinking about it in days to come). We'll run through a few possibilities here, but these are designed primarily to spark your own ideas. Ideally, what you put on the list will be something that only you would have thought of. Get creative.

Public speaking. It's said that people fear it almost as much as death. If you're going to confront this fear, start in a more casual atmosphere—take a speech class, or practice telling a complete story or long joke in front of a small group of family and friends. Then "ramp up" to a N.O.W. experience: renting a theater stage to put on a once-in-a-lifetime solo performance (Your life story? Your favorite jokes?) in front of family and friends.

Heights. Start with small steps, literally—by going up a ladder. Make yourself stay up there for a little while; get used to looking down at the world. Then take it to a higher level by enrolling in mountaineering camp (for more on mountain climbing, see chapter 5).

larly the grouper that was being fed to them then. "See that," I said to Shane, "they don't care what you or I taste like. With all due respect, Shane—they don't give a damn about you." He nodded and kept looking only at me for a while longer, but finally he couldn't resist the amazing sight beneath him. He turned his head, looked down, and literally faced his fear. And I think I detected a smile on his face.

Airplane flight. If you've got this fear, you absolutely *must* beat it because it's cutting you off from the full possibilities of travel and thereby keeping you from leading a N.O.W. life. Start by educating yourself on how planes actually work and why they're so safe. Consider joining a group like Fly Without Fear, whose members meet weekly. Go to a flight-simulation center, where you can get the feeling of being in a plane while still grounded. After you've flown a few times, consider ramping all the way up to a skydiving experience—because once you've jumped out of a plane, sitting in one is easy.

Snakes. Find out the facts: How many are really dangerous? Do they really want to go after you? Take it in steps after that: First, look at snakes from behind glass (at a zoo, aquarium, or conservatory). Then seek out an opportunity to actually touch a snake in a supervised situation with a snake handler present. Ramp up to a N.O.W. jungle experience.

Claustrophobia. Believe it or not, putting yourself in the closet actually does help (though if someone walks in on you, you may have some explaining to do). In my own case, I ramped up by going into caves, then diving in underwater caves.

4

GET LOST

ON THE ROAD TO SELF-DISCOVERY, THROW

AWAY THE MAP.

THERE IS NO HIDING from technology, it seems. Your cell phone and laptop make you "reachable" wherever you go. Your credit card purchases are electronically tracked, as are your Web site visits. Your drive across town is plotted in advance by MapBlast!, and should you get the sudden impulse to veer off that predetermined path, the Global Positioning System in the dashboard will second-guess you. Progress is a wonderful thing.

But have you ever thought about just getting away from it all? Ditching the BlackBerry, throwing away the map, and purposely taking yourself "off the radar"? I get this urge every so often—a reaction, I suppose, to being exposed to too much media, too many day planners, too much talk about Google. It makes me want to go somewhere refreshingly out-of-touch, someplace strange and tranquil. I get a hankering to, for example, go hang with an indigenous tribe.

Such was the case one day a while back, when I decided to pay a visit to a Yekuana village. I would have called to let them know I was coming, but they don't have phones there. Or mail. The way you tell the Yekuanas you're coming to visit is by cupping your hands over your mouth and emitting a loud, high-pitched chirping sound. They hear that sound coming from downriver and they instantly know that it's either you or a capybara, the world's largest rodent, approaching.

To get to the Yekuana village I visited, you fly to Caracas, Venezuela, then take a short hop in a biplane. Next, you follow the road on the map that leads straight to Chincheros. At this point, you can get rid of the map, because it will no longer be helpful. The only thing to do is get into a dugout canoe and paddle into the uncharted heart of the Venezuelan jungle. This I did with a local biologist named John and another local named Fernando, who liked to be called Tarzan.

When we came upon a little clearing where a long, sleek handmade canoe rested on the shore, John nodded. "*Yekuana* means 'canoe-builder,'" he explained as we pulled our boat to shore. This was one of the most virgin areas left in the world, John told me, virtually untouched by anything modern; through much of its history, it was sheltered from outsiders by surrounding rapids and waterfalls that made it hard to reach. Leaving the boat, we followed a dirt path to a row of straw huts. Children stood and watched us, wide-eyed. The adult tribesmen were a little startled at first, but several of the men soon welcomed us and sat us down at a long, elegantly carved table for some liquid refreshment. What it was I have no idea, but it did quench my thirst and did not kill me.

After resting up, we set out to do what the Yekuana do pretty much all the time: We took a canoe ride away from the huts and the women and children to go do some hunting and fishing (without guns or fishing rods, mind you). I assumed a couple of tribesmen would join us, but in fact about eight of them squeezed into the small boat; I thought it might capsize right then and there. No one wanted to be left out. "We do everything to-gether," the tribe's chief explained to me by way of John's translation. The chief was not a formal guy at all—no fancy headdress, just a rag tied around his head. He seemed young for a chief, about 30, but then again all the Yekuana seemed young (maybe time really does stand still there?).

The boat ride was quiet and peaceful. A couple of red and green macaws sailed above, peering down at us. Downriver, we disembarked at a favorite hunting spot. And over the next couple of leisurely hours, we sat under-neath the trees and tried to shoot birds off the branches with spit-darts. These were tiny arrows carved from sticks by the tribesmen, who inserted them into one end of a long bamboo tube. The idea is to blow hard in the direction of the bird. Some of the darts missed the mark, and the tribesmen laughed hysterically when this happened. Some darts glanced harmlessly off the birds' wings. Just when you were wondering how these guys ever ate, a shot would land true and bring the bird crashing down. I gave it a try, and I can tell you it's not easy to hit the bird. I did manage to disturb a nearby hornets' nest and ended up with a sting in my elbow, but a tribesman quickly helped me draw the venom out and we all had a good laugh.

By this time, the chief had moved from hunting to fishing, using a stick carved to form a spear. He skewered a stingray and showed it to me proudly. Later he caught a bunch of piranha and showed me those, too, urging me to feel how sharp their teeth were. This would be our dinner a few hours later, back at the huts. The fried stingray was very tasty; the piranha soup was, let's just say, interesting (teeth and all). After dinner and relaxation, it was back out in the canoe again, where we literally whistled in the dark—the whistle was intended to lure the capybara out of hiding. This is just one more way the Yekuana differ from you and me: *We* would probably be inclined to *avoid* a 100-pound rat. That night, we caught only a baby one—the little fellow couldn't have weighed more than 15 pounds, scarcely big enough to qualify as a rodent in these parts. We eventually sailed home to the huts under a night sky of brilliant stars, content that our work was done.

In the morning, I sampled a local species of termite for breakfast and was surprised to find that it tasted like lemon. We took another lazy canoe ride under a gorgeous blue sky framed by jungle trees. Feeling a burst of energy, I decided to scale one of those majestic trees—climbing

GETTING LOST IN EXTRAVAGANCE

Going primitive and giving up your comforts is one way to get lost. But you can also go the other way and see what it feels like to live among the privileged tribe—if only for a day. Wealthy people experience luxury all the time and barely appreciate it. You, on the other hand, can afford to do it only once—which means you will revel in it.

- Become a high roller for a day at a casino. You'll see what it feels like to get the royal treatment.
- For one season, become a high-level donor at your local theater or radio station. For the next few months, you'll be treated like a VIP, invited to exclusive parties and special performances.
- Rent a top-of-the-line luxury car, and make it a convertible; drive around like a rich guy, if only for a day.
- Stay in The Waldorf-Astoria in New York City for one night and order room service.
- Get a group of your friends or business associates together and charter a private jet. And be sure to drink champagne on board.

higher than I've ever gone in a tree, until I was 100 feet up (Fernando helped me climb, and I could see why he was called Tarzan). Resting at one of the top branches, I saw the whole rain forest laid out beneath me in all its multihued magnificence. I think I could have stayed on that little perch forever, surviving on fruit and maybe the occasional termite. And if I had stayed, I can assure you of this: No one in the "civilized world" would have had any idea where to look for me.

MY BRIEF STAY with the Yekuana tribe was probably one of the most memorable adventures I have ever experienced. There were no big

PROOF THAT YOU CAN *STILL* GET LOST ON YOUR BIKE

Recently, *No Opportunity Wasted* was contacted by a couple of cowboys who like to saddle up on bicycles. Andrew Herringshaw and Daniel Hattaway are known for taking over empty fields in their home state of Oklahoma and putting on bike races that feature hairpin turns, steep jumps, and screaming fans. But like a lot of adventurous bike riders, they had an urge to find a new and "cool" place to ride. They chose the remote, frozen outpost of Barrow, Alaska. Located 340 miles above the Arctic Circle, it is about as close to the "top of the world" as you can get. Andrew and Daniel's plan, with help from the N.O.W. TV series, was to fly to Barrow, meet up with the locals (a small, primarily Eskimo population of 4,000), and organize the world's northernmost bike race—*on ice*.

It's easy to feel "lost" in a place like Barrow: With no roads leading in or out of the town, no cell phone service, and a culture adrenaline-rush activities (even that tree climb was relatively tame by bungee standards), no whirlwind itinerary, certainly no fancy accommodations. And yet I felt completely alive and engaged every moment of the experience. I think it's because I was totally out of my element. I had abandoned the world I knew and fallen into one that was strange and fascinating. I was "cut off," in the best sense of that term, yet I was also connected—to the natural world, to living at the most basic level, and to a group of fine people, the likes of whom I'd never seen before and perhaps never will again. I was sampling and experimenting and learning the whole time. All because I was completely and wonderfully lost.

steeped in old Inuit traditions (whaling season is the "main event" in these parts), it's a long way from home for two extreme-biker dudes in cowboy hats. Initially, the locals were a little baffled by the outsiders and their strange ways: For example, Andrew and Daniel spent their first day in town setting up a bike race course on ice and using 1,000 half-inch screws to make studded tires for the bikes. When it came time to organize the race, the cowboys weren't sure whether the locals would join in or whether they'd be able to ride bikes well enough to make the event interesting. But maybe Andrew and Daniel should have realized that when it comes to doing *anything* on ice or snow, an Alaskan has an edge on an Oklahoman. The cowboys were soundly defeated in their own race. Not that they minded: Andrew and Daniel got a crash course in Inuit culture, made a townful of new friends, learned that hairpin turns are even hairier on ice, and returned to Oklahoma with a fond appreciation of southern heat.

And so if you ask me what I think should be prioritized on your List for Life, ranking a close second behind that initial challenge of facing your fear, I'll tell you what I tell many people (and please don't take it the wrong way): *I think you should get lost.* It is not very hard to achieve; some of us do it without even trying. There are thousands of interesting ways to get lost, which we'll get into as we look at some possibilities. Most important, it is something you *need* to do—something you probably crave, though you may not realize it.

You don't have to go halfway around the world to get lost. What I'm talking about is a simple two-step process.

1. Put yourself in a situation or environment that is completely novel and removed from your everyday experience, and then . . .
2. Allow yourself to become immersed in this world and just . . . go with the flow.

By this definition, getting lost might involve going only as far as the other side of town—*if* you can find some kind of exotic experience or faraway world there and *if* you're willing to temporarily lose yourself in it. By doing this, you expand your horizons, open yourself up to new influences, and test your own resourcefulness and adaptability. Getting lost can be a great way to broaden and strengthen yourself, in addition to providing an unforgettable experience.

WHY "GETTING LOST" GETS A BAD RAP

So why does the very thought of getting lost make some people flinch? Because generally, it is associated with messing up: misreading instructions, failing to plan ahead, having poor instincts or bad judgment. It can be a source of panic in some, embarrassment in others. Think of the man and woman driving together who suddenly find themselves uncertain of where they are. If they behave according to stereotype, the woman will immediately want to pull over and ask for help (panic), and the man will steadfastly refuse to do so (embarrassment). We've gotten so used to being completely in charge and in control of our environment and our own comings and goings that any temporary loss of that control is seen as intolerable, unacceptable, and inexcusable.

But too much control and not enough mystery can be deadening to the soul. It can dull your natural instincts for adapting, coping, surviving. There's something deep inside us that *wants* to get lost every once in a while. It's tangled up with the genetic need to seek out and explore (the aforementioned Gene Wild, rearing his unkempt head again). In fact, exploration—which most of us would consider a good and worthy thing—cannot really be separated from the act of getting lost. Not to sound too Zen about it, but it's plain fact that you must first get lost before you can begin to discover and find.

Children seem to "get this" better than adults do. Think back to when you were given your first bike: If you were like a lot of kids, you probably started riding around the block, covering familiar ground. But gradually you wanted to expand your boundaries, and you instinctively knew that the only way to do that was to just . . . *ride*. Let's try a left here, and maybe a right up there, and see where it leads; in other words, you purposely got yourself lost. And though it may have been a little scary, it was good for you, and undeniably thrilling—a freeing experience. The first time my friends and I took our bikes out into the bush in Antigua, we rode down into a mysterious valley where everything took on a different hue. We became completely disoriented. We

In Case You Have to Eat a Bug . . .

One of the great things about getting lost in a strange place is the experience of eating strange things. I love doing it because I consider exotic eating to be a memorable experience; when I eat something bizarre, that taste tends to stay with me (for better or worse) for years. I think it gives you a better sense of what a culture is like when you eat what they eat. Plus, I just like to test myself: It's not easy putting something into your mouth that looks like nothing you've ever seen before, and it can be even harder with something you *have* seen before—perhaps wriggling in the dirt. My own personal rule is, if you don't know that something is safe to consume, don't eat it. But if you can ascertain that at least two people have eaten this thing in the past and are still here to talk about it, then bon appétit. Here are a few of my favorite snacks.

- Grasshoppers (with peanut butter)
- Piranha

loved every moment of it. And I still recall the details, almost 3 decades later.

But responsible adults tend to have a harder time pushing themselves to venture out without a plan and a detailed itinerary. Even when we travel to exotic countries, we try to minimize the risk of becoming disoriented. We plan out every leg of the journey, leaving no room for sudden detours; we travel in groups of our own kind, largely separated from the locals; we seek out lodgings that offer the comforts of home; we gravitate toward familiar oases ("Hey, look, there's a Starbucks!"). You can always tell the dif-

- Possum soup
- Cobra blood
- "Huhu grubs" (These little white bugs are plucked from trees, and you eat them by holding the head and the anus and biting into the middle.)
- Green ants
- Scorpion canapés (Actually, I haven't tried these yet, but they're on my list; the plan is to eat them before they eat me.)

If you're serious about insect cuisine, there are restaurants that now serve these delicacies (Typhoon Restaurant in Santa Monica, California, has water bugs, crickets, and Manchurian ants on the menu). You can also visit the popular Hokitika Wildfoods Festival in New Zealand (www.wildfoods.co.nz). One caveat: When you eat adventurously, be prepared for the occasional queasy stomach. However, I must say my own track record is such that at the Wildfoods Festival, I have come to be known as "Cast-Iron Keoghan."

ference between a traveler who is truly embracing the journey and one who is trying to control it, limit it, homogenize it. The latter person will arrive in a place like Vietnam and demand that breakfast include the butter and jam he's used to having at home. You hear him cry, "You don't have strawberry preserves? Are you sure? But that's what I *always* have for breakfast!" People like this may have traveled halfway around the world, but in their expectations and attitudes, they're still stuck back at home. And they want the world to conform to *their* ways and peculiarities. In contrast, the travelers who know how to get lost and become immersed in another world realize that *they* are the ones who should be doing the adapting. They welcome the challenge of trying something new.

FORSAKING COMFORT

This leads us to what is perhaps the first and foremost point to make about getting lost: To do it well, *you must be willing to give up comfort.* Crazy as it may sound, you should actually *look forward* to giving up comfort for a little while. Comfort is a constant in our lives today. We have too much of it—in our plush-seated cars, in our home-theater dens, and right down to our soft walking shoes. Giving up some of it for a little while won't kill you. It'll only make you stronger.

And it will make you appreciate the comfortable life you presently take for granted, by reminding you how damn good you have it. To me, one of the more wonderful aftereffects of "getting lost" somewhere strange and challenging is that you eventually return to your old familiar world with a newfound appreciation for even the smallest things. After spending time in a place where you can't get a decent shower, you come back and suddenly a shower isn't just a shower anymore—it's a kind of miracle, an experience to revel in and savor for a good half-hour. On *The Amazing Race*, I think the line I've heard people mutter more than any other is, "I can't wait to get home and sleep in my own bed." You can just picture them diving into that bed the first night back, rolling around and luxuriating in the wonders of a Sealy Posturepedic. That first night home in bed becomes an experience, a N.O.W. moment—made possible by the fact that they've spent the preceding month having a "sleeping experience" that involved floors, beaches, benches, and airplane seats.

The willingness to make yourself uncomfortable extends beyond physical comforts to emotional ones, too. When you're in your emotional comfort zone, you always have the feeling of being in control. But when you get lost, you have to let go of that feeling. You become the proverbial "fish out of water," and there can be any number of emotional discomforts that go with that. For example, you may be the type of person who never wants to appear helpless, but unfortunately, the fish out of water is bound to flop around and look a little desperate at times, and may even (gasp!) have to ask for help from strangers.

You may also be the kind of person who likes to remain inconspicuous. But when you immerse yourself in a strange environment, you suddenly become the "different" one, and that can make you stand out. As someone who has spent 3 decades engaging in fish-out-of-water activities, there are two things I can tell you: Number one, people will go out of their way to help you when they see that you've been willing to lose yourself in their world. And number two, the more you thrust yourself into other worlds, the more you'll start to *like* that feeling of being different and conspicuous. It's much more satisfying than being invisible.

TAPPING INNER RESOURCES

Of all the benefits of getting lost, here is the biggest: When you place yourself in an unfamiliar environment and force yourself to adapt, you use and stretch muscles that have probably been languishing for a while. This includes the ability to:

- Learn new skills quickly (as in, how to shoot a dart through a tube and hit a bird to get dinner).

• Fend for yourself with only the resources at hand. On one level, this might mean living among people as they live, simply. On a more extreme level, it can mean going off on your own into the wild and trying to survive.

• Rely on spontaneity and instinct to navigate a path. This is the point at which you call upon your inner pioneer, who just loves to go "off the map" and blaze fresh trails.

Tapping into these resources can help you in all aspects of your life, and in ways you'd never imagine. For example, if you immerse yourself in a strange culture or environment and force yourself to cope with daily challenges, "it sharpens your sensitivity to behavioral signals," says Nella

How to Enjoy Being Lost

This will sound "New Age-y," but here's the secret: Getting lost is all about being "in the moment." That means you have to try to turn off the part of your brain that's always worrying about what comes next, what time it is, where you'll eat, and how the heck you're going to find your way home. You can worry about that later, but while you're lost, try to just . . . be lost. Focus on what's going on around you, not what lies ahead. Allow yourself to be "carried along" by the experience and the people you're with. If you need a mental image, use one. Water works for me: Just let yourself flow. Water always ends up somewhere, eventually. Along the way, trust your own instincts. But at the same time, don't be afraid to ask people for guidance and help; it's a great way to deepen your immersion.

Barkley, of the human resources consulting company Crystal-Barkley. "You learn to figure out how a cultural system works, how to read people's body language, how to engage them to get what you need to survive."

You also learn how to make the most of what's available to you in any given situation, and how to do without—realizing that you're tougher than you might have thought. And maybe most important, you can, like the child on the bicycle, come to terms with the idea of getting lost, embracing the sensation of temporary disorientation—that "lost" feeling—without automatically becoming alarmed or panicked. If you can do this, it will help you in countless situations: every time you travel, every time you change jobs or move to a different neighborhood, or go into a strange restaurant, or sign up for a class with a group of people you don't know.

There is also a pride that comes with knowing you can get yourself lost for a while and find your way back whole. Most of us, even if we're living a very comfortable life, want to believe we're capable of adapting and surviving without those comforts. Have you ever noticed how people love to tell you how tough they once had it? "Well, I know what it's like to do without," they'll say, "because when I was growing up 40 years ago. . . ." At this point, I like to cut them off and remind them that 40 years was a *long time ago*. What comforts have you given up lately? Regardless of how hard you may have once had it, if you don't ever leave the shelter of your *current* lifestyle, your edge has been dulled. And you've probably lost your appreciation of the simple life *and* the soft life. Only by going back and forth between the two worlds, and experiencing the difference, can you fully enjoy and appreciate both.

TAKING THE FIRST "MISSTEP"

So how do you begin the process of getting lost? Start with small steps—or we might call them "missteps," as in deliberately stepping off your own beaten path. You can start as simply as taking a different route home from work one day, a more roundabout one that takes you through areas you may not be familiar with. If you're really feeling bold, make an unplanned stop and get out of the car and stroll.

Lunch hours are also a great time to get lost for a little while. Forget

BACKPACK ESSENTIALS

If you're planning to get lost for a little while, be sure to pack for the trip. Here are some useful things to carry in your backpack, according to Dennis Lewon, equipment editor at *Backpacker* magazine.

- Compass
- Lighter
- Bottled water
- An extra layer of clothing
- Sunscreen
- High-energy snacks (energy bars, dried fruit, nuts, beef jerky)
- Small pocketknife
- Lightweight rain jacket or poncho
- First aid supplies
- Mosquito repellent (if you're going to a buggy area)
- Lightweight tarpaulin (to sit on or to provide temporary shelter in a rainstorm)

the company cafeteria or the nearby deli or diner you've worn out. Go a little bit out of the way and find a small ethnic restaurant that seems intriguing (and if you like it, strike up a conversation with the people who run it; now you're beginning the immersion process). I also recommend taking a bag lunch to a park where you've never been, preferably one with a hiking path. As you walk down that wooded path, be on the lookout for detours off the trail—maybe a nice little spot with a tree that's great for sitting under. Now take this lunchtime excursion to the next level: On a weekend, pack a few things in a knapsack, then get in your car and head for the nearest wilderness area. You're allowed to use a map to get there, but *not* once you're there. Explore the place by wandering. Do your damnedest to get a little lost, and then use your own instincts to find your way out.

These small forays are just the warm-up for something bigger: dream number 2 on your List for Life. Some possibilities are listed in the box on pages 88 and 89, but as with everything on your list, try to be original, and try to think of something that has special meaning to you. Think of peoples and cultures that have always fascinated you, places that seem so different and strange that they intrigue you and scare you a little at the same time. Think of ways you can temporarily "cut yourself off" from the life you normally lead—perhaps by giving up certain comforts, abandoning habits. And of course, needless to say, leave the cell phone at home. Where you're going, it probably won't work anyway.

GET LOST: POSSIBILITIES

There are so many ways to get lost, it's hard to know where to begin. Here are a few general guidelines accompanied by a few specific suggestions.

Join a tribe. This is one of the best ways to lose yourself: When you join a tribe, if only for a short time, you can't help but be swallowed up and immersed in a strange new way of life. I recommend going to Lake Titacaca in Peru to participate in the locals' annual week of celebration and mourning, or going on a walkabout with Australian Aborigines, or going hunting with the nomadic Kazaks of Western Mongolia. If that seems out of reach, keep in mind that even the place where you live has tribes—people who have formed their own groups and observe their own cultures and traditions. Motorcycle riders are a tribe; so are tornado chasers; so are nudists; so are people obsessed with Wayne Newton. If one of these tribes fascinates you, go spend time deep in their world for a while. Look for weird annual conventions that speak to something in your soul, and crash that party for 4 days (Did you know there is an annual convention for ventriloquists? And one for twins? And one for yodelers?). Whatever tribe you choose, the key is to join in; don't just stand on the sidelines gawking.

Look for the remote. No, it's not between the sofa cushions. To find the most isolated spots on Earth, you must be willing to take multi-legged journeys over very bumpy roads. But it's worth it. Here's a possibility that I heard about, and now it's on my own list: checking into one of the most remote hotels in the world. It's in Papua New Guinea, and to get there you have to take a big flight, followed by a little flight, followed by an 8-hour bus ride, and then a trek through virgin forest, using a compass as your guide. When you reach water, throw away the compass, get into a canoe, and hope for the best. You'll know you're getting close to the hotel when you encounter members of a certain ancient tribe who will point in the direction of the hotel as soon as you look at them.

Get marooned. The idea is to deposit yourself on an island that feels truly cut off from civilization. If you want to do this right, live like a castaway: no fancy hotel, just a hut or bare-bones cottage or maybe even a tent. Catch your own fish and cook it over an open fire. Put a message in a bottle and set it afloat. Become Robinson Crusoe. And if you want maximum authenticity, consider going to Robinson Crusoe Island, a remote Pacific island 500 miles east of the Chilean coast, where Alexander Selkirk (the real-life model for the Crusoe character) was marooned for 5 years. The island includes Selkirk's original home—a small cave, accessible only by water.

Go on a "quest." This term has been used to describe a type of journey in which you follow an unusual path with a particular goal in mind—as in retracing a famous trip someone once took, or adhering to a quirky theme, such as searching for the lost tribes of Irian Jaya, looking for covered bridges throughout Wisconsin, or stopping in at every 100-year-old pub in Ireland. Here's a great example of a quest, submitted to our TV show by one of the N.O.W. dreamers: Carl Nunziato wants to travel to Poland to try to follow the route taken in the 1930s by his grandfather, Zeno Kowalezcko, who fled on foot during the invasion of Poland. (Zeno, 15 at the time, walked through the Carpathian Mountains to Russia, got a boat to Europe, and went on to live a long and fruitful life as a doctor in the United States.) What's great about a quest is that it allows you to lose yourself in an idea, a bit of history, or a quirky subculture of other "questers" who care passionately about something.

5

TEST YOUR LIMITS

"I have always admired the ability to bite off more than one can chew and then chew it."

—WILLIAM DEMILLE

THIS WAS THE MOMENT Mike Orsini was waiting for—and dreading. He stood hunched in the goal, his face sweating behind the hard mask, his right hand squeezing the goalie stick. Speeding down the ice toward him was an opposing player with wide eyes and a puck cradled in the bow of his stick. The boisterous crowd went quiet: 5,000 people collectively holding their breath. Mike could feel all eyes on him, and not just those watching in the arena. This had turned into a media event, and he was at the center of it, with TV news cameras trained on him to see how "Everyman" would measure up in this moment of truth. His coach and teammates on the bench stood and yelled encouragement. Somewhere up in the stands, his girlfriend covered her eyes, unable to look. The fast-approaching shooter pulled back his stick and unleashed a fierce slap shot. The puck went airborne, screaming toward Mike at about 90 miles an hour.

And in that long second it took to reach him, he had to be asking himself: *What's a 49-year-old postal worker doing in a spot like this?*

Here is the answer: Mike Orsini wanted to test his limits. Like a lot of us, he wondered about his own capabilities and fantasized about having a chance to put it all on the line. On the surface, Mike seemed like an unremarkable guy: He'd spent the past 20 years pounding the same mail route in Rochester, New York, and on weekends he indulged his childhood passion, hockey, by fooling around in a local men's league. Like a lot of weekend jocks, Mike harbored a suspicion that there was a serious athlete deep inside him: someone quick, skilled, fearless, and capable of playing hockey with the best of them. *Maybe.* The only way to know for sure was to let that inner Gretzky out on the ice for a day, put him in front of *real* players, and see if he could stand his ground.

And so one day in early 2004, instead of just delivering letters, Mike sent one. "My dream is to play a professional hockey game as a goalie," he wrote to *No Opportunity Wasted.* He laid out his vision of how he planned to make this happen: Find a minor-league hockey team willing to give a dreamer a shot, train intensely with that team in the 2 days leading up to his big game, then step in front of the net and let the pucks fly where they may. He believed in his heart that he would play well. And if not, he wrote, "the fans will get their money's worth by heckling me."

After I received Mike's letter, I encouraged him to begin contacting teams, which he did. But nobody even bothered to respond to him; they probably figured it was a joke. He was about ready to give up when he got a call back from, of all places, Huntsville, Alabama. Yes, they do play hockey in Alabama. They play it so well, in fact, that the Huntsville Channel Cats had this crazy notion they could still beat their opponents even with an untested 49-year-old mailman as their goaltender. With the Channel Cats on board and ready to give Mike a shot, I paid a surprise visit to Rochester to tell Mike that N.O.W. was prepared to back him on his quest. When I arrived, Mike was officiating a local hockey game and was shocked to see me come out on the ice, stepping gingerly in my sneakers. "Are you ready to do this dream now?" I asked him, with witnesses in the seats all around. He laughed and then nodded. I told him he had exactly 3 days to get his rear end down south, get into game shape, and get in goal.

Mike had no idea what was waiting for him down in Huntsville. First, he was poked and prodded by the team's doctor, and then he had his legs stretched to the breaking point by a physical therapist. They informed him that he was not quite in the great physical condition he imagined ("But I walk a lot," Mike protested). They explained that he would have to summon all his strength and more just to fend off exhaustion on the ice. And somehow, some way, he was going to have to move faster than he'd ever moved in his life to keep up with the breakneck pace of the game. "But don't worry," the doctor reassured him. "If anything happens, I'll be ready to stitch you up."

Once the doctor and physical therapist finished with him, it was on to practice, where Mike suited up in his hockey uniform (he was thrilled to see "Orsini" stitched on the back) and stood in goal to be pelted by pucks. His teammates—all in their early twenties and tickled at having an old-timer in their midst—seemed to be holding back on their shots, which angered the coach. "You're not doing him any favors by going easy on him," the coach told them. Asked after practice about the challenge Mike would face the next day, the coach tried to be upbeat, saying that if Mike could survive the first 5 minutes, he might be all right. More specifically, if he could deal with that first shot—that first bullet to the head—then maybe, just maybe. . . . Then the coach shook his head and laughed. "Mike really has no clue what he's in for," he said.

As the game approached and word of the story got out, all four

Huntsville TV stations wanted to interview Mike, and he became a hot topic on local radio. "What he's doing," said one disc jockey, "is every guy's dream." By the night before the game, Mike was feeling the pressure. Still, he had no reservations, no thoughts of pulling out. He told me, "I am not going to go through my whole life without knowing what it feels like to have a 90-mile-an-hour puck coming at me."

FOR MIKE, THIS WAS NOT just some fantasy sports moment, or a chance to play "star for a day." He needed to find out something about himself. Only by testing the limits of his abilities at the very highest level could he satisfy his basic need to know: Am I good enough, tough enough, brave enough, smart enough? How much can I take? How do I measure up?

We've all asked ourselves those questions at one time or another, though perhaps not lately. Putting yourself to the test is a big part of growing up, finding out what you're good at, and competing for your place in the world. But as we settle into adulthood, we tend to avoid such trials and tryouts. We like to think we've moved beyond that. After all, we've established who we are—and we don't have to prove anything to anybody. Right?

Well, not quite. Maybe it's true that we're past the point of trying to gain the approval of parents, coaches, teachers, peers, or even (if we're lucky) bosses. But it seems we never outgrow the desire and need to prove something to ourselves. On *The Amazing Race*, on *No Opportunity Wasted* TV, and basically anywhere I go, I am constantly encountering people—of all ages and all levels of accomplishment in life—who still feel that burning urge to demonstrate to themselves that they can do it (whatever it may be). This is not a sign of insecurity or immaturity on their part. On the contrary, I believe it is the best of human nature at work. Yes, here again we're talking about Gene Wild.

(continued on page 96)

REACH FOR THE SKY

The great British explorer George Mallory was once asked why he wanted to climb Mount Everest, and his famous answer was, "Because it is there." But I think the real reason people are driven to climb mountains is twofold. First, climbing a mountain represents perhaps the ultimate (or at least the grandest) way to test our limits, by seeing just how high we can go. And I think we also do it because we want to gain a different perspective on the world around us. If only for a short time, we want the view from the top.

Both reasons are compelling, which is why I think mountain climbing merits serious consideration on your List for Life. One of the best experiences of my life was a trek up the Andes a few years back. It took 4 days to climb to the 15,000-foot peak, and, of course, getting there was half the fun. For the first 3 days, donkeys carried the gear, and our group bonded as we climbed, sharing stories, laughs, and meals of dried goat meat. I added one additional item to my diet, though some of my fellow climbers were reluctant to join me. I'd learned from local villagers we met on the way up that if you chew on coca leaves, it can help prevent altitude sickness (in other words, getting high helps as you get higher). Perhaps because I'm so used to getting lost around the world and relying on the wisdom of local people, I followed this advice without question. And who knows, maybe it "heightened" the experience in some ways. All I can say is, when we reached a mountain pass at 10,000 feet and I realized we were now above the clouds, I began to feel that I had truly separated myself from the lowly and mundane life below. (Unfortunately, the spell was briefly broken—and I was reminded how hard it is to *completely* rise above earthly realities—when in this remote, cut-off region we came upon a local mountain man wearing a Chicago Bulls jersey.)

On our last day, we left behind the stubborn donkeys—they believe in upward mobility, but only to a point—as we began the difficult final ascent. The experience kept getting better as we went up. Well, it did for me, anyway: My partners were feeling the altitude sickness by this time, but I was immunized and ecstatic. When we reached the top, everything was dead quiet except for the sound of our own shoes on the rock and the flapping wings of giant condors cruising past us. Instead of being tired, I felt exhilarated as I looked around, able to see farther than I'd ever seen before. There was something wonderful about knowing that, at this moment in time, no one in the world stood higher than we did.

The Andes experience only makes me want to go even higher, of course; such is the escalating addiction of mountain climbing. Everest is on my list, and so is New Zealand's own majestic Mount Cook, which I plan to climb with my 62-year-old father. The thing to understand about mountain climbing is that anyone can do it, though you have to choose your mountain appropriately. If you're serious about going to the absolute pinnacles of the world, you'll need instruction and training (start by checking in with a group like the American Mountain Guides Association, www.amga.com, which accredits guides and climbing schools). But there are lots of mountains that are accessible to climbers without technical skills. Even my Andes climb could have been done by anyone with strong legs, a willing spirit, and a supply of coca leaves. If that climb is too steep for you, scale back to a smaller mountain, or even a hill. *Anyone* can climb *something*. Start by surveying the area where you live, setting your sights on the highest point visible. Then go climb to that point. And when you get up there, take a deep breath, look around, and enjoy the view.

That same instinct that pushes us to explore also makes us want to be tested. The two impulses are different but related. When we "get lost" or explore, we're pushing boundaries outside ourselves; when we test personal limits, we're pushing the boundaries within us. For the person who had the original Gene Wild, this distinction was perhaps insignificant: He or she wouldn't have survived without pushing both boundaries.

WHY WE CRAVE HARDSHIP

The modern world is very different, of course. It rarely sends wildebeests charging at us to test our agility, strength, and resourcefulness. And without those daily tests, we get soft and sluggish. We're aware of that softness, and we don't necessarily feel good about it. We understand, deep down, that we were built to be tried and tested. Hence, we have the longing to test ourselves, which we act on . . . occasionally.

But we don't do it often enough, hard enough, or in ways that are interesting and stimulating enough. Our self-imposed tests tend to become predictable routines: A 1-mile morning jog, a half-hour at the gym three times a week. I'm not knocking this: It's always a good idea to stay in shape. But workouts are often designed to maintain limits that have already been established (for example, your proven ability to jog a mile). If we really want to satisfy the primal urge to be tested, we must push ourselves to another level—one we've never attained before, one we may have assumed to be beyond our capability.

Obviously, a test like this can take many forms, some more physical than others. But whatever form it takes, an ultimate test should demand that you shed blood, sweat, and tears (well, maybe no blood). It has to be hard, or it won't be truly meaningful. This doesn't mean, however, that the experience can't be enormously fun, too. In fact, the ideal "Test Your

Can You Handle . . . Plato?

Testing limits doesn't have to be about physical challenges. We're just as hungry for mental tests. How about putting yourself up against the neighborhood's best in a chess competition? Or signing up with the local debating society? And here's a thought: Instead of trying out again for your old basketball team or reentering a foot race you once lost, what about trying to wrap your head around an academic subject that was too much for you to handle back in those lazy school days? You could, for example, revisit physics. Or see if you can finally get a handle on trigonometry. Or learn German. Or read James Joyce's *Ulysses*. But here's my suggestion: Give yourself a crash course in philosophy, and see if you can keep your brain from collapsing under all those weighty thoughts.

Ready for your first workout? One, two, three, go: "There are two sides of philosophy, the theoretical and the practical," says Tom Morris, author of *Philosophy for Dummies*. "The theoretical side addresses 'The Ultimate Questions': Does God exist? Is there an objective difference between good and evil? What is the meaning of life? The practical side of philosophy tackles issues of everyday life: What is true success? What is real happiness and how can I experience it? For the theoretical questions, Plato is a good place to start. If you want to understand what motivates people to ask philosophical questions, read Plato's essay 'The Apology.' You may want [to read] all Plato's dialogues, or at least to sample a few like 'The Meno' (what do we owe society?) and 'The Phaedo' (life after death). Aristotle is harder to read, but his *Nicomachean Ethics* is a good starting point. The famous Descartes experiment in discovering the foundations of knowledge can be found in his *Meditations*. On the practical side, get a translation of the *Meditations* of Marcus Aurelius. Next, read some of Ralph Waldo Emerson's essays. Then, consult the *Tao Te Ching*, an ancient Chinese text of wisdom, or *The Analects of Confucius*."

Limits" challenge for you—the one you'll begin thinking about now, and the one that will soon be written on that third line of your List for Life—should be a trial you're eager to prepare for, a test you just can't wait to take. It should thrill you as you're doing it, and upon completion it should leave you both thoroughly spent and totally elated—falling to your knees as you pump your fists to the sky. That's a N.O.W. moment.

SEEKING OUT TESTS

Where on Earth can you find a challenge that will bring you this level of satisfaction? Everywhere. There are so many possible ways to test yourself, the issue is not finding one but narrowing down the options to find the best one for you. For starters, there are many examples of what might be called "generic" tests—races, marathons, walkathons, boot camps, survival courses—that are open to anyone willing to sign up. I wouldn't suggest just randomly choosing one of these events for your N.O.W. list, because I tend to think the choices on your list should have some personal significance to you. But it may well be that a particular marathon or event does have some significance to you. Perhaps the locale fascinates you, or the history of the event, or the fact that your grandfather once took part in it.

One of the plans on my own List for Life these days is to compete in the Hawaiian Ironman triathlon, a grueling race that combines running, swimming, and biking. It's a dream for me because in my conversations with athletes through the years, that event has often been held up as a gold standard of fitness—which has always made me wonder if I could do it. But on top of that, one can't discount the fact that . . . it's in Hawaii, dude! What could be better than an event that makes you burn up and then drops you into the gorgeous blue Hawaiian waters? My feeling is, if you can blend a task you feel driven to do with a place you dream about visiting, that's a recipe for a *No Opportunity Wasted* experience.

UNFINISHED BUSINESS

But in addition to considering more generic tests and events, it's a good idea to look for a challenge that hits close to home—one that has some deeper connection to your life. Over the past year, I have encountered a number of N.O.W. dreamers who are driven by the idea of taking on a challenge from their past: something they wish they'd done years ago, or something they attempted once and failed to complete. For example, we heard from two men who, years ago, participated in the famous Eco-Challenge race. They failed to complete the race because of a subpar performance, and they've been haunted by that failure ever since. They believe that the best way to test their limits is to reenter that race and finish it this time—which they plan to do soon, quite possibly with the *No Opportunity Wasted* TV cameras recording their efforts.

Others have come to us with similar "unfinished business" requests. We heard from a man who, years ago, had been enrolled in Special Forces training to become a Green Beret. Because of an injury, he had to pull out of the training program, and now he wants to return to the place where he trained and put himself through a new physical test. Another dreamer told us he wanted to go back and finish his Navy SEAL training; his failure to do so 20 years ago has remained "the biggest letdown in my life," he wrote to N.O.W.

This burning desire to go back and retake an old test from the past is important to people because "if you don't do it, you can end up living with regret for the rest of your life," says *Men's Health* magazine's Joe Kita, whose book on this very subject, called *Another Shot*,

NO LIMITS, EXHIBIT A:
SISTER MADONNA BUDER

I was feeling pretty proud of myself at the time: Competing in a mini-triathlon down in Florida a few years back, I finished my race in what I thought was a respectable time for a fellow pushing 30. Then someone told me about the nun. She wasn't in our little race—she was in the bigger, harder one, a full-scale Olympic triathlon that was part of this same event. She was biking, running, and swimming twice as far as I was. And by the way, she was in her mid-sixties at the time.

That was my introduction to Sister Madonna Buder, who has over the past 2 decades continually competed in—and won—various Ironman events around the world, often setting records for her age bracket. Today, at age 73, Sister Madonna still competes, as she continues to defy limits of all kinds. Women are not expected to excel at "Ironman" events, and yet she does. People her age are supposed to be losing stamina, but hers just seems to grow. And nuns are not supposed to be athletes at all, but she's a magnificent one.

Affiliated with the Catholic Church in Spokane, Washington, Sister Madonna spends much of her time serving the community but manages to take part in several triathlons each year. She didn't begin running seriously until she was almost 50 years old, but she was soon up to 4 miles a day. Then she set her sights on the Boston Marathon, followed his own efforts to go back and retake old tests, including a tryout for his old high school basketball team. At age 40, Kita actually returned to the school and asked the coach to allow him to compete for a spot on a team he'd been cut from more than 2 decades earlier.

which she ran in (and completed) in 1982 and then again in 1983. Sometime after that, she got the idea of competing in triathlons after reading a newspaper article about the sport.

"I figured, well, I've done marathons, and I know how to swim, and I used to ride a bike as a child—so why not give it a try?" she says. She overcame a couple of serious bike accidents and broken bones during her early Ironman efforts in the mid- to late 1980s. But she kept going strong through the 1990s, competing in the 60-plus age bracket. One of her most impressive performances came in a 1992 triathlon, in which she stopped to help a dehydrated competitor and comforted the woman until help arrived—then completed the race and still broke the record for her age bracket.

Sister Madonna shows no signs of slowing down, and currently has set her sights on a new Ironman record for her age bracket (70- to 74-year-olds). This is just one of a number of life goals she hopes to achieve (for a look at her List for Life, see chapter 11). To older people thinking about taking up demanding physical sports, she advises, "I think you always have to listen to your body, because it will tell you what you can do and how far you can go. Be patient in the beginning. Try running just a block, then walking a block, and then running another block. Set a modest goal for yourself each day, and keep building. If you have the desire and you think you can do it, you *will* do it."

He had no intention of playing with the team but just needed to know if he could make the cut. I asked Kita why this was so important to him, and he told me, "Being cut from that team was something I never got over. It was crushing to me. And I always believed it was a mis-

NO LIMITS, EXHIBIT B:
JESSE BILLAUER

Among the hundreds of dreamers' letters that have come to the head-quarters of *No Opportunity Wasted* was one from a surfer dude named Jesse Billauer. Like a lot of surfers, Jesse dreams of finding himself curled inside the perfect wave—or to use his jargon, he wants to "get barreled in a tube." That's hardly surprising, and ordinarily his letter wouldn't have stood out. Except for that one line in the letter where he mentioned—almost in an offhand, "by-the-way" manner—that he is a quadriplegic.

Eight years ago, as the 17-year-old Jesse was on the cusp of breaking through as a top surfer (he'd already been cited as a hot prospect by the national surfing magazines), he suffered a stunning setback. He had decided to go surfing with some friends in the morning, before school. A wave surprised him from behind, knocking him down and compressing him face-first into a sandbar. He felt his body go limp as it floated to the water's surface, still facedown. Jesse couldn't even turn himself over to breathe. Fortunately, another wave came in, this time flipping him over. He called to his friends for help.

His spinal cord injury left him with no sensation or movement below the middle of his chest and only limited use of arms and hands. When you think of the limits that can be placed on a person, *this* is the real deal.

take—that I should have been on that team." The only way for him to resolve this matter, Kita said, was to go back and correct the mistake. At the end of a tough 2-week tryout period ("I was sore every day," Kita said), the coach gave him the results: You would not make the

But almost immediately, Jesse began to push against those limits by remaining active, learning to do simple tasks and then progressing to more-difficult ones. Of course, the one thing he wanted to do most was surf. And about 4 years after the accident, with help from some friends, Jesse got back on his surfboard. He had to be carried out to the wave and then helped onto the board, lying on his stomach. "When I first tried it, I didn't really have enough strength to stay on the board for very long," he says. But he has gradually built up strength and now is able to ride waves better and longer.

When not riding waves, Jesse can be found giving motivational speeches at schools and youth events as part of Life Rolls On (www.liferollson.org), a nonprofit foundation he started in order to promote awareness of spinal cord injuries. Part of his message includes telling young people, "Whatever obstacle you face, don't give up. And whatever you want to do, do it now—because tomorrow is not guaranteed."

Jesse is following his own advice: Among the dreams he's pursuing (and N.O.W. is presently working with him to try to make it a reality) is a trip to the Mentu Islands in Indonesia, where he will try to ride the biggest waves he's ever taken on, in a dreamlike setting. "To me, it's the perfect place to surf," he says. "It's a lot harder than the kind of surfing I'm doing now. But it would be an amazing experience, so I feel like I have to try it."

starting five, the coach said, but you would definitely make the team. "I was so thrilled to hear that," Kita said. "And the experience gave me the confidence to go back and try other things I hadn't done in a long time."

The fact is, if you've ever tried to do something and come up short, what you're left with is a limit: a defined point beyond which you are (supposedly) unable to travel. That limit might as well be posted on a sign in your head that says: *"Don't bother trying to do that. You tried once and failed; therefore, we know you can't do it."* Maybe you're the only one who sees this posting, but it's a powerful inhibitor that can keep you from ever reaching your full potential. That's why I recommend that as you look for ways to test your limits, look first for those personal limits—see if there are any such signs posted in your own psyche.

A limit, by the way, can be put in place not only by experiences of failure but also by other factors that have nothing to do with your own actions or capabilities. If you are a person of a certain age, or gender, or physical condition, you may bump up against limits placed on you by others—preconceived notions about what you can and can't do. Some of the most inspiring people to me are those who, like Sister Madonna Buder or Jesse Billauer, are constantly testing those limits and pushing right past them.

PREPPING FOR THE BIG TEST

As stated earlier, whatever limit you choose to push, whatever type of challenge you take on, the one common denominator is that it should be hard to do. And that means you'll need to prepare and train for the test. To do anything less is not only a recipe for failure but is also reckless and irresponsible. If you try to go from zero to 60 too fast, you'll only end up hurting yourself.

How you prepare will of course depend on what the particular test is, but the general rule is, start slow (particularly if you haven't been involved in that type of activity for a while) and build steadily. You may need to put yourself through some form of structured, supervised training program, or you may be able to design and follow your own program. If you opt for the latter, consult with experts beforehand: your doctor for starters, but also perhaps a trainer at a nearby health club or (best of all) someone who has experience preparing for the type of challenge that's on your list.

The training process itself becomes the first exercise in testing limits: Every day, you should be pushing that barrier of what you can do by an extra yard, or one more pushup. In my own workout program, I've found that it's invaluable to have someone around who helps to push you past "the wall"—the point at which you're inclined to stop doing something because you feel tired. The more times you push yourself past that wall, the more you begin to realize that the wall is both passable and movable.

If you've trained well, you should be ready for the test. But it is *still* going to be one of the hardest things you've ever done. There will come that moment—it always comes if the test is truly a test—when you begin to doubt that you can do it, finish it, or survive it. I can recall this moment with utter clarity when I think of various tough tests I've undertaken, such as the time I ran a race known as the "GutBuster" (a 7-mile run with a 1-mile stretch going straight uphill, which is the gut-busting

(continued on page 108)

HELL ON EARTH (ALSO KNOWN AS PHIL'S WORKOUT)

Talk about testing your limits: Racing around the world in 30-odd days on *The Amazing Race* is tough on everyone, including the host. A typical race can span 75,000 miles, 6 continents, and up to 25 cities, all in the span of a month. You find yourself traveling by plane, train, bus, ship, canoe, foot, rope (as in rappelling), or, on occasion, rickshaw. Sleep is a rare commodity; nutritious food can be hard to come by. You have to be pretty durable to make it to the end. During each race, I have some strict rules for my body: no alcohol or coffee (I don't want any stimulants because I need to be able to sleep at a moment's notice on a train or plane). Sometimes instead of sleeping, I'll try to meditate while flying; it's a good way to recharge my battery in a short span. And I drink *a lot* of water at all times throughout the race.

Before each race, I put myself through an intensive training program, overseen by a mean and heartless personal trainer who shall remain nameless. He runs a small, un–air-conditioned sweat box in Los Angeles, and each time I walk into that gym, I know that he is going to push me as hard as I've ever been pushed. Sometimes, in the midst of training, I find myself wishing that bad things would happen to this fellow. He insists, however, that he's doing it all for my own good. Here's his explanation. (Notice the unsympathetic tone).

"I know where that wall is for Phil, the point where he wants to quit. I also know he can go much further than that. It's like that with most people: That point you get to where you're feeling tired and you have to stop—that's not even close to your limitation. Often it's not even half of what you can do. But you need someone to push you past that wall. If you don't have a trainer, get somebody else, maybe get your wife to yell at you. Somebody has to tell you to keep going. And not listen to your pathetic excuses. When Phil tries to give me those

excuses, I tell him I don't want to hear it. Then he'll say, 'I hate you,' and I say, 'That's nice. Now give me twenty more.'"

The workout changes constantly, to condition different muscles. It doesn't require much in the way of equipment: a jump rope, a pair of dumbbells, boxing gloves, and a strong heart. Here's a fairly typical workout (if you're going to try this, start slowly and carefully).

- Jump rope for 15 minutes, to warm up.
- Dumbbell punches: Holding a 5- or 10-pound weight in each hand, punch straight out, anywhere from 100 to 200 times with each hand.
- Squat thrust/front kick: This one's a killer if you do it enough times. Drop to the floor on your hands, kick your legs out behind you, bring them back, jump to your feet, and deliver a high, hard front kick. (This works best kicking a sparring partner with focus pads, or you can kick a heavy bag.) Immediately, drop down and repeat. Do 10 fast repetitions; 20 reps just may floor you.
- Squat thrust/three-punch combination: Same as above, but when you rise, you punch (left-right-left combo) instead of kicking.
- Killer pushups: In standard pushup position, lower your body until your chest is inches from the floor. Slowly, move torso to your left and hold for a beat, move back to the center, then move to the right and hold, then move back to the center and push up. Okay, that's one. Now do 10 of those.
- Hand-walking: In the lowered pushup position (chest near the floor), walk on hands and feet. Go forward 25 feet, then turn around and come back.
- Situp crunches: Try to get to 100. Then see if you can get to 200.

In a 1-hour workout, I try to do all of the above in multiple sets, never breaking for more than a couple of minutes between sets.

part), or the time I swam from Europe to Asia across the Bosporus Strait. Often, that critical moment of truth comes about midway through the challenge. If you get past it, you're likely to get a second wind that can take you within view of the finish line—at which point momentum carries you home.

But first you must get past that moment. At times like that, I feel as if there are two voices talking to me, one over each shoulder. On one side is "Mister I Can't," telling me to pull over, it hurts too much, and it's hopeless because I'll never finish anyway. "Mister I Can't" has a very seductive voice. Meanwhile, there's a harsher voice coming from over the other shoulder, saying: *"I don't want to hear it. If you're not dead, then you have no excuse for stopping."* That's the guy I try to listen to, even if he is a cruel and heartless bugger.

THE "F" WORD
(AS IN *FAILURE*)

But what if, after rigorous training beforehand and all your best attempts during the actual challenge, what if, in the end, you simply can't pass that test? We will speak of this remote possibility only briefly here and then never again—because if you want to push limits, the word *can't* simply can't be in your lexicon. Of course, there's the possibility, especially if you've set a very ambitious challenge, that you could come up short of your goal in some way.

But if the test you gave yourself was ambitious, memorable, and meaningful, you don't necessarily have to have passed with flying colors. It will still be an outstanding experience in your life. Just putting yourself on the line enough to even attempt such a difficult test places you miles ahead of most people and should be a source of enormous pride. And whatever the result, you have answered that "What if?" question burning inside you. You had the guts to find out how far you could go. Was it only three-fourths of the way? Well, that's not a failure; that's a new benchmark for you. Now you know that you can get at least that far. That's a limit you can choose to accept as reality (no more of that "I wonder if . . ." speculation). Or—and this is the option I'd recommend—it's a limit you can choose to push a little further, on another day, in another test.

Of course, maybe, just maybe, you will completely nail that test the first time out. Maybe you will find that when the moment of truth arrives, fast and hard like a 90-mile-an-hour puck, everything will come together for you: instinct, training, determination, and perhaps even a touch of luck. Instead of flinching, you will react with blinding speed— and your gloved hand will snatch the puck out of the air as the crowd erupts in cheers.

That's what happened with Mike Orsini when that first wicked slap shot came at him. The coach, the players, and the fans couldn't believe it when they saw it happen: It was a save worthy of an all-star goalie. He made a dozen more saves before the game was over, en route to a 5-to-1 victory for the Channel Cats. Mike had the performance of his life. Later, in the locker room, he received a "Player of the Game" award from his coach, but before that, just as the game was ending, Mike went to center ice and took a microphone in hand. He asked his girlfriend, who was sitting in the crowd, to marry him (she said yes). It's a funny thing about testing limits: Once you start, you can't seem to stop.

TEST YOUR LIMITS:
POSSIBILITIES

Go the distance. The idea is to take something you like to do and do it *longer, farther, more* than you've ever done it before. Here's a simple one: Set your own personal walking record (but to liven it up, choose an interesting route that takes you through the length of your town, and while you're at it, let the folks in town know you're doing this—maybe they'll cheer you on and give you free refreshments as you stroll by). The same principle works with a bike ride, though you can go much farther and choose *really* interesting routes. I like this idea from Deborah Johnson of Detroit, who told N.O.W. she plans to use her bike to retrace a 200-mile stretch of Harriet Tubman's Underground Railroad, running from the banks of the Ohio River to Windsor, Ontario.

Test your tolerance. I love the idea of seeing how much discomfort I can put up with. Why do it? It's like pounding your head against a wall: It feels so good when you stop. One possibility is to see how long you can last in a sauna (if you find out you're really good at it, consider signing up for the Sauna World Championships). Then, of course, there's the old favorite, walking on coals, which is on my list of things to do. I'm told it doesn't hurt because the perspiration on the bottom of your feet absorbs the heat—as long as you step lightly and don't loiter. If you prefer cold to heat, try "ice diving." Or you can just take a dip with your local Polar Bear Club.

Audition your heart out. Try out for the lead role in a theatrical show in your town; better yet, try out for a role that requires you to sing and dance. Try out for a sports team that you have no chance of making; train like hell beforehand, so that you *do* have a chance. Best of all: Audition for the circus.

Report to boot camp! Tiger Woods did it, so why not you? Recently, after completing the Masters Golf Tournament, one of the world's greatest athletes decided that even *he* needed to shape up—so he quietly enrolled in an authentic Army boot camp program. Boot camps run the gamut from semi-tough to downright merciless: If you're looking for the latter, try to make it through the Team Delta boot camp, run by ex-military commandos. No one has ever lasted 3 days. But hey, you could be the first!

Take fun to the extreme. By adding an insane twist, you can turn routine everyday games and sports into a survival test. For example, in Australia I played Speed Golf, described as the most dangerous golf game in the world. Here's how it works: one ball for each team, four players per side. You whack from the first tee while the second player runs ahead and tries to hit the ball as soon as it lands. At the same time, the third player is running ahead to follow up on that shot (keep in mind that all of these runners must avoid getting *hit* by the ball). The fastest team to sink the putt wins that hole. (By the way, we did this in 120-degree heat.) I thought this was pretty extreme until I learned recently about André Tolmé, who golfed his way across Mongolia using a 3-iron. For Tolmé, this was both a way to test his golf limits and a way to "get lost" in exotic terrain once crossed by Genghis Khan. Other variations on this extreme sports theme include subzero football, rainstorm baseball, and fireball soccer (you douse the ball with lighter fluid, set it aflame, then play with bare feet; apparently, this is a hot sport in Java, Indonesia).

6

TAKE A LEAP OF FAITH

I'M NOT AN UNHAPPY MAN, and yet I like to jump off bridges. And throw myself out of airplanes. And if you take me to a cliff, I'm liable to strap on some form of artificial wings and then run toward the precipice at full speed—until there's nothing but air under my feet.

It's not enough that I do these things to myself; sometimes I pull others over the edge with me. A while ago, I visited New Zealand, the country that gave birth to both bungee jumping and me (coincidence? I don't think so). I rounded up seven innocent people and convinced them that they should jump off a bridge with me. Why do such a thing? Because as best as I could determine, nobody had ever done it before. People had been eccentric enough to bungee jump in clusters of five or six, but that's all. I don't think anybody had tried seven. And in case someone might be considering it, I upped the ante by going for an eight-man jump. Just to play it safe, so to speak.

Together, the eight of us went to the same bridge where, in 1989, this crazy activity was first commercialized. The term *commercialized* is probably more accurate than *invented*, because who really knows when people might have started jumping off things with some type of line tied to their feet? For instance, there was an ancient ritual called *naghol* that for centuries was practiced on the tiny South Pacific island of Pentecost. It involved leaping from great heights with vines tied around the ankles and was done to test manhood and to fertilize the earth below. But the people of Pentecost never tried to make a global business out of it. That started in New Zealand, specifically in Queenstown, where a couple of adventurers named AJ Hackett and Henry Van Asch happened upon a dilapidated bridge that extended over a deep gorge.

Hackett had already experimented with cord-jumping from the Eiffel Tower a year earlier, but in New Zealand, Hackett and Van Asch joined forces to try to turn this into a business. Van Asch took some of the early test dives, including the first "moonlight jump." He bound his own feet together with a latex rubber cord that was attached to the bridge. The drop below was between 130 and 165 feet; the cord was a little shorter than that. Van Asch shuffled to the edge of the bridge after midnight, in pitch darkness. And then he just . . . jumped. He plummeted down face-first. Logic told him that the cord, once fully extended, would stop his fall and save his life. But of course, he didn't really *know* that the first time he jumped; the technology was still relatively untested. And of course, he could see nothing in the darkness. Still, Van Asch had faith, and that faith was rewarded with a sudden and sharp jerk. His body at that point stopped falling and began rising, then fell again, and then bounced up again, like a yo-yo on a latex rubber string. After he was hauled to safety, Van Asch reportedly said, "I think we are on to something here."

And they really were. Those first solo jumps helped launch a New Zealand company that would eventually attract more than a million visitors from around the world, and soon other companies offering the same service sprang up worldwide. An offbeat little industry was born and today continues to attract hordes of people, all lining up and paying their money to experience that feeling of powerful uncertainty that Van Asch felt on his first moonlight jump.

And people do get that feeling, certainly the first time they jump, probably the second and third, and maybe the fourth. Around about the 10th time, the rush isn't quite as strong because it's no longer the leap of faith it once was. By that time, you know deep down what the outcome will be; you know all too well that you're going to live. It is at this point that some people who are hopelessly addicted to the sensation of leaping into the unknown might tinker with the experience by adding a new wrinkle, such as trying an eight-person jump. It's an attempt to get back to the unknown by doing something that hasn't been done before, much like Van Asch's moonlight jump. Who knew whether an eight-person jump could really be done? I thought it could, but did I know for certain? Was there actual proof of survival? Because there wasn't, it qualified in my mind as a leap of faith and a thing worth trying.

So it was that the eight of us stood at the edge of a platform on that bridge, with our toes pointing to oblivion. Among this group was none other than Henry Van Asch. An old friend of mine, he helped accommodate my dream of attempting a record-breaking jump and then decided to join in himself. Even after all these years and countless jumps, he still can't resist trying one that might bring a slightly different rush. We all locked arms with each other to form a human wall. I was on the end and used my free arm to hold out a video camera, pointed back at us to capture the expressions on our faces as we fell.

"So, on three-two-one," I announced, "we've *all* got to jump, right?" I was just making sure we were a unified front, and we were (though someone grumbled, "Whose idea was this, anyway?"). Then I asked Henry, "Should we keep holding on to each other all the way down?" He thought that would be worth trying, though gravity might have other plans that would break us apart. One thing was certain: We were all going off that edge together. When you join arms with eight people, you lose the freedom to change your mind at the last minute; if you don't jump, you'll be pulled. That didn't bother me. I was happy to have my fate intertwined with this particular cheerful group, whether for the next 8 seconds or (worst-case scenario) for eternity.

As it turned out, it was just for the 8 seconds, though it always seems longer than that. A bungee jump, or any type of free fall, so greatly intensifies the experience of living that each second is densely packed. You'll see more expressions on a human face in those 8 seconds than you might see over the course of a month. My camera captured all of the shifting emotions during the drop, including wide-eyed anticipation (*This is going to be so cool.*), creeping dread (*Well, it'll be over quick.*), sudden shock (*Whoa—did we really just jump off a bridge?*), clenched-jaw determination (*I will survive, dammit.*), existentialist doubt (*What if I cease to be?*), cautious exhilaration (*Hey—I think we're having fun now!*), brief curiosity (*So how's everybody else doing?*), pure pleasure (*Who cares if I die, this is worth it.*), abrupt panic (*Wait—is that the* ground *rushing at us?*), sensory overload (*Cannot process; must shut down.*), startled reawakening (*Who's yanking on my feet?*), immense relief (*So glad that's over.*), a touch of regret (*Is that all there is?*), and finally deep self-satisfaction (*All hail the Bungee King, as I dangle upside down before you!*).

EIGHT SECONDS OF SHEER MADNESS and then, just like that, it's over and you're left upside down and twirling on a string. So why do it? Just for the momentary thrill? Well, that's part of it, of course. And not an insignificant part, either—momentary thrills should not be taken lightly. They end up comprising much of the highlight reel of your life.

And sometimes their effects last for more than just a moment. When you spend time around people who have parachuted, bungee jumped, or rappelled down the side of a mountain for the first time—and I happen to be around such people quite a lot on *The Amazing Race*—you get to see the full effect of such an experience, not only while it's happening but afterward. If I didn't know better, I'd think some of these people had just taken an incredible drug that made their skin glow as they smiled uncontrollably and recounted the experience for an hour, or two, or maybe for the next day and a half. My own feeling is, when you can get this kind of a powerful "high" legally and naturally and without killing off brain cells, there's something to be said for it.

But there's another reason that I think all of us should be willing to take a leap of faith from time to time, and why I believe this is an important theme to consider when creating your List for Life. It's about more than just enjoying a temporary thrill. The leap of faith, in its various forms, is what carries us past uncertainty to the other side of the unknown. And to make that leap, you must summon a belief in yourself: the faith that you'll be able to defy gravity and do whatever it takes to end up safely on your feet.

Having this faith in yourself—and having the will to act on it by taking that leap into the unknown, again and again—can serve you well at every kind of chasm or cliff you may encounter in your life. When faced with a dramatic life change, a difficult choice, an opportunity that has great potential but no guarantee of a successful outcome, the leap of faith is often the only way forward. Of course, we can, in many such instances, choose *not* to leap. We can say, "That's insane! Who knows if I'll make it across? Or what it will be like on the other side?" We can back away from the precipice, choosing to stay on safe ground while others go ahead and make that leap. This is a choice some people tend to make throughout their lives. And in so doing, they never get to experience life

WHEN YOU'RE HURTLING THROUGH THE SKY, REMEMBER TO . . .

Keep your eyes open and look around. It can be scary at times, but you don't want to miss a thing. "Let your mind catch up with your body," says skydiving champ Dale Stuart, who explains that people in the act of parachuting may tend to feel more rushed than they should. "You have a lot of time before you have to do *anything*. So take that time to relax and collect your thoughts."

Breathe. It'll help you relax.

Be aware of your body. If your leg is bent or your arm is in a weird position, it can steer you in an unwanted direction.

Don't obsess about the pull-cord on your parachute. You'll know when it's time. And if you somehow fail to pull it (for example, in the highly unlikely event that you pass out), a safety backup device will cause the chute to fire automatically. You'll also have a reserve chute if the first one doesn't work.

Watch out for other flying people. Skydivers tend to flock together. This becomes an issue as you stake out a place to land; make that spot your own. And try not to change your landing spot at the last minute.

Forget everything you've just been told. That's not an order, it's a prediction: When you're free falling, everything leaves your mind, including advice. You exist only in that moment—which is part of what makes it so great.

on the other side of the great divide, the one that separates those who say, "I'll jump" from those who say, "I think I'll just stay put."

To live a *No Opportunity Wasted* life, you *must* be willing and able to make leaps into the void. It's the only way to get to the other side of the chasm, which is where so many great opportunities and experiences await you. Of course, there are many ways to leap across that chasm; you certainly don't have to bungee jump or skydive. I happen to like those two modes of transportation, and I believe they can help to stretch and strengthen you for other, very different types of leaps.

But in a more general sense, almost any activity that requires a big, bold step away from safety and into the realm of risk (usually more of an emotional risk than a physical one) can be thought of as a leap of faith. This can, for example, take the form of:

- Jumping with both feet into a movement you've long believed in, but were wary of getting swept up in

- Finally taking the plunge after years of hovering at the edges of doing something ambitious—for example, painting that long-discussed masterpiece, making a film, opening the little shop on the corner you've envisioned for so long

- Just swinging out on your vine to try to meet new people or make a fresh start in a new environment—not knowing if you'll be accepted on the other side

MY BIGGEST LEAP

In my own life, the biggest leap of faith I ever took wasn't off a bridge or a cliff. It was a step off an airplane, albeit one that had already landed safely on the ground in New York City. I had come all the way

AN ATTEMPT TO RATIONALLY EXPLAIN THE APPEAL OF BUNGEE

I know it seems like a crazy thing to do. But here's my own view on why bungee jumping is so damn much fun. One minute you're totally secure and you feel gravity holding you on the earth. At this point, your fate is in your hands. You decide to leap. And then, for a moment in time, you are weightless in space. You assume that fairly soon, the bungee cord is going to pull you up. But until that happens, you don't know for sure if you're going to live or die. Suddenly, there is no security in your life. This may sound like a bad thing, but it's not. You gain a newfound appreciation of the life you've taken for granted all these years. You become hyperaware of the world around you as it rushes by. All of your earthly worries and problems evaporate except for one: staying alive. Just as you begin to experience "ground rush"—which is like staring death in the face, though only for a couple of seconds—you're pulled back from the brink. Salvation! You feel that sense of control and security slowly returning to your life. A switch goes on inside you, announcing, "You're okay; you've survived." And at that moment, you're overcome with a sense of relief. This causes a powerful emotional release, expressed in the form of a deep primal scream that you never knew you had in you. And that's it. Now you're ready to return to the office.

from New Zealand with my future wife, Louise, and we were determined to make a new life in a new country. We had no job, no prospects, no idea how it would all turn out or whether we'd land on our feet. All I knew was, I wanted to work on a TV show in the United

BEFORE YOU JUMP
THROUGH THAT CLOUD . . .

I thought I'd share this bit of advice from my own skydiving experience, because I wish someone had told me. Ever find yourself looking out the window in an airplane and seeing soft, puffy clouds? Ever think about how much fun it would be to jump into, and then sail through, one of them? That's what *I* thought, until I tried it. I leaped out of a plane directly over a soft, puffy white cloud. I had ethereal visions of floating around inside that cloud, perhaps stopping for tea with an angel. But when I got inside the cloud, three things happened.

1. Whiteout. You can't see a thing. It's like the worst blizzard you've ever been in, except . . .
2. It was actually more like an ice storm. Clouds are made of water, and if it happens to be chilly, as it was on this day, those

States. But I quickly found myself in a classic catch-22 situation: I couldn't get a green card unless I had an agent, and I couldn't get an agent unless I was in the television union, and I couldn't get in the union unless I had a green card.

The only solution Louise and I could think of involved taking a second leap of faith, almost as big and blind as that first step off the airplane. We decided to try to independently create a TV show pilot, which we would then try to sell to a TV distribution company, which (if we succeeded) would enable me to attain professional status, get into the union, and get a green card. This was akin to bungee jumping without the cord. It was crazy to think that we could create a TV show (we had no money, no particles of water become little bits of ice, which pelt your face as you are traveling through at 120 miles per hour. So much for the angels; it felt like I'd been welcomed by a hive of angry bees.

3. Disorientation. Because you can't see anything when you're inside the cloud, you lose track of where you are in relation to the earth. Even knowing what the cloud ceiling is before you jump, once you're inside the cloud you begin to wonder how deep it is and how close to the earth. There's no way to tell until you come flying out the bottom. At that point, the world suddenly reappears—a lot closer than it was before you went into the cloud. You look back up at the cloud you just left, and it's shrinking quickly, which makes you realize how fast you're going. It's quite scary.

The point is, clouds are not as gentle as they might seem.

camera crew) or that anyone would want it, if and when we finished making it. But we took that first step into the void anyway.

I sought out some people with camera skills who were hungry for work, and I convinced *them* to take a leap—by working without pay in the belief that something would come of all this. (One of those people, Scott Shelley, is still doing camera work for us today, more than a decade later, proving that a little leap can have lasting consequences.) Once we had a crew, we had to come up with a story to film. We happened to encounter a fascinating man named Jim McMullen, who'd written a book about his own adventures tracking and trying to save the endangered Florida panther. It was easy to see that McMullen would be an interesting subject: A Vietnam veteran who'd fled down to the jungles of the Everglades to escape civilized life, he seemed to identify with the noble panther-in-hiding. We asked McMullen if we could come down and film him as he tracked the elusive animal. To my surprise, he said yes.

Soon thereafter, I followed McMullen into the Florida swamps, and this, too, required a leap of faith. When you step into those swamps—infested with alligators *and* snakes—there's no guarantee of coming out in one piece. At one point, my cameraman, Scott, and I were up to our armpits in the muck, with gators splashing all around us. McMullen calmly talked us through it; I knew instinctively that this was someone to be trusted when it came to surviving in the swamps. (Another good lesson here on leaps of faith: Sometimes you must have faith not only in yourself but in others who can help you make the leap, though you may have to rely on your own instincts and judgment to determine whether such people really are experts worthy of that trust.) McMullen eventually led us to the beautiful, regal-looking panther, and we left with rare footage and the makings of a fine little pilot TV show.

From there, it all came together, like a soft, easy landing at the end of a parachute jump. We found a distributor who was interested in the show; his interest enabled me to get my green card; and having the green card as well as a pilot under my belt helped me land my first job with a U.S. TV network. But it never would have happened without all those sequential leaps into the unknown, starting with that very first one that took me away from the safe, familiar ground of New Zealand.

THE FIRST STEPS

If you haven't been taking a lot of leaps in your life to this point, it can be tough to suddenly begin doing so. You have to start to build and strengthen the "leaping muscle." But first, there's something very important to know about this muscle: *It is located in your mind, not in your legs.* One of the people who taught me this was the aforementioned Henry Van Asch. As you might imagine, Van Asch has closely observed thousands of people on the verge of making a leap. And what he has concluded is that the leap takes place entirely in the heads of these people. There is almost no physical requirement in bungee jumping—you simply have to show up and then step out. Once you begin falling, there are really no physical demands on you, because gravity and the bungee cord do all the work. There is also almost no risk of injury, and no one has ever died on one of AJ Hackett Bungy's million-plus jumps. "And yet," Van Asch points out, "people mistakenly think of this as an extreme sport that's both hard to do and dangerous." All it really is, Van Asch explained to me, is a decision to try something—"a mental leap and nothing more."

That "mental leap" is what you must work on and practice if you're going to get better at taking leaps of faith. It is, quite simply, the ability to give yourself the "full speed ahead" command when the temptation might be to hold back because of uncertainty. If you want to exercise this muscle, you can start small; there are countless opportunities in daily life to take tiny leaps of faith. Any time you initiate conversation with a stranger, any time you agree to possibly look foolish by trying a sport or activity you haven't tried before, any time you invest in someone or something with no certainty of payback (a friend in need? an underdog in a race?), you're taking a little leap. And every little leap helps you to become more comfortable with risk, thereby preparing you for bigger leaps.

Once you've tried a few of these "everyday" leaps, progress to one that is a little more extraordinary. This is where something like a bungee jump, a skydive, a white-water rafting excursion, or even a roller-coaster ride can be useful. These and similar "white-knuckle" activities may not

(continued on page 126)

TAKING A "LIFE LEAP"

In many cases, the dreams you write on your List for Life may tend to involve "outside interests"—activities or experiences that are removed from your workaday life. But that doesn't have to be the case. There may be some instances in which your N.O.W. dream has a direct connection to your work or daily life. And this could certainly be true when it comes to "taking a leap of faith."

If you've been thinking of making a dramatic change in your daily life—perhaps starting a new business, or packing up and moving to a new place, or changing tracks in your career—this can require a leap of faith that makes a bungee jump or skydive seem mild by comparison. When you take one of these "life leaps," you're not playing, and there's no parachute or latex rubber cord to keep you from crashing. To take such a leap often requires you to have tremendous faith in your dream and your abilities. You may have to put a lot on the line, with no solid promise of successful results.

But I see people take these kinds of leaps all the time. On a recent airline flight, I met a fellow passenger who told me the tale of how he maxed out his credit cards and risked financial ruin, all so that he could launch an arcane product that nobody had ever heard of and few people could understand or appreciate. (Specifically, he devised a system that involved putting elaborate blinking lights on animals to be able to distinguish one from another in certain situations. Does that sound like something you'd bet your life savings on?) Today, the product and the company, Pet Blinkers, are hugely successful. But there was no way of knowing that in advance, and in fact the chances originally seemed slim.

This is often the scary scenario faced by entrepreneurs, inventors, artists—anyone who is creating something new. Because it's new, there is no way of knowing if anybody really wants it. You just have to *do it* (launch it, build it, create it, or write it) before you can find out if there's going to be a payoff. This runs counter to the way that most people are used to working. Typically, we demand a guarantee that we're going to get paid back if we invest time working on something. We want a contract, a paycheck; we want assurances that our time will not be wasted. But often you must forgo all of that when you decide to take an entrepreneurial or a creative leap. Similarly, a move to a new town or country, or to a new industry, is fraught with the same kinds of risks; the whole thing could turn out to be a waste of time and money.

So how do you decide if it's worth the risk? I believe each "life leap" opportunity has to be judged individually, with some thought—but not too much—devoted to the likelihood of success. The *real* determining factor, in my mind, is passion. If you feel incredibly strongly about this idea, this move, this opportunity, if you feel driven to do it . . . then you almost *have* to take the leap, or you'll always regret it. And if your passion is that strong, it will give you the strength to make a solid go of it even in a tough situation. Your passion becomes your parachute, in a sense. It'll keep you from crashing early, giving you a chance to find your footing.

If you leap for reasons other than passion—to try to make a quick buck, for example—it can be a mistake, notes Jeff Bezos, who took a huge leap himself when he started Amazon.com. Writing about entrepreneurship in a recent issue of *Inc.* magazine, Bezos advised dreamers against jumping into a business venture just because it's perceived to be a "hot" opportunity. "If you're really interested in medicine and you decide you're going to become an Internet entrepreneur because it looks like everybody else is doing well, then that's probably not going to work. You don't choose your passions, your passions choose you." So instead of chasing a wave, he says, "find that area that you are interested and passionate about—and let the wave find you."

represent your ultimate leap, the one you'll write on your list. But they can serve as great ways to ramp up and build nerve.

WHAT'S IN *YOUR* POOL?

As for the leap that you choose to write on your N.O.W. List for Life, it should be a significant one, of course—not just in terms of the breadth of the chasm you're trying to cross, but also in the depth of meaning this particular challenge has for you. Think of a diver on the edge of a diving

LOOK BEFORE YOU LEAP

If you're skydiving, bungee jumping, paragliding, or taking any other leap that involves some physical risk, it's important to check out the credentials of the operations offering these services. When considering a skydiving program or school, see if it is affiliated with the leading national organization. In the United States, that would be the U.S. Parachute Association (www.uspa.org). Group-member skydiving centers have pledged to follow basic safety requirements, including use of proper equipment and training by USPA-rated instructors. The U.S. Hang Gliding Association (www.ushga.org) certifies hang-gliding instructors and schools; for lists of certified schools, visit the Web site. Bungee jumping is less regulated, but there are local organizations, such as the U.S. Bungee Association, that have set down guidelines adhered to by reputable operators. Your best bet might be to make sure the company has been in business for at least a few years. I'm all for after-dark leaps, but not with a fly-by-night operation.

board who cannot bring herself to dive into the pool: If that diver is you, then *what is in that pool?* What is the leap you've always wanted to make but never could bring yourself to try? If you can identify what's in the pool, you've found a strong candidate for item number 4 on your List for Life (and if you can think of more than one pool that you wish you'd jumped in through the years, choose the Olympic-size one: Go for the biggest, boldest possibility). As you're considering all the possibilities, by the way, don't limit your thoughts to fun and games or leisure activities. It may turn out that the leap that belongs on your list pertains to your everyday life, perhaps a major career move or a "dream business" you would like to start.

Once you've written this dream on your list, you may be tempted to take that leap right away. That's a good instinct, but don't be in too much of a rush to leap too soon, and don't do it blindly. As I've said previously in other chapters, there is *always* time to prepare and lay the proper groundwork for an experience; those preparations should be seen as part of the overall experience. In particular, if the leap you have in mind involves physical risks, do your homework to ensure safety. Likewise, if you're jumping into a new cause, career, or all-consuming project, spend some time learning more about what you're getting into; this will only increase your chances of a happy landing.

But don't overthink it, and don't make the mistake of believing you can eliminate all risk through endless analysis and hemming and hawing. If you linger too long at the edge of the precipice, you can become paralyzed. Give yourself a definite timetable—and when it's time to jump, don't allow yourself any excuses or outs. If it helps, you might want to consider bringing seven people to the edge with you. You can all lock arms and count down together, and when you get to "one," there'll be no chance of holding back.

Leap of Faith: Possibilities

Dance on air. Skydiving is a fine thing to put on your N.O.W. list, but it is a tad generic. If you want to enrich the experience and make it more individualized, consider adding "freestyle" moves to the dive. This is something you can easily try once you've taken a few beginner's dives and gotten comfortable in the air. Freestyle diving involves creating your own dance moves or just striking interesting poses while you're in the air. Dale Stuart, a former world champion freestyle skydiver, says that beginners can simply make up their own moves or look for inspiration by checking out pictures of other freestylists (Stuart's Web site, www.winddance.com, offers pictures and basic how-to instruction). Once you've experimented with a few moves on your own, do what the pro freestylists do: Bring along a fellow jumper (it can be a friend or someone you hire) to shoot video footage of you on the way down, documenting and preserving your "air dance" forever.

Glide with the wind. The best thing about paragliding is that when you're up there sailing through the sky, it's wonderfully quiet—as if you've been closed off in your own world. There's also a sensation of being at one with nature, because the wind is the only thing holding you up. Surprisingly, it's not scary once you get up into the wind; you feel very stable and protected. The experience can be even more spectacular if you take off from a scenic cliff, as I did when I glided solo off the cliffs of Chile, soaring across a pristine desert and facing out on the Pacific Ocean. I wanted to stay up there forever.

Go ballooning. Maybe you're not the skydiving type. In that case, riding in a hot-air balloon gives you some of that same thrill of being in the sky with no airplane walls closing you off from the birds and clouds. If you want a particularly dramatic balloon experience, consider taking off with thousands of other balloonists at the Albuquerque Balloon Fiesta. For a time, you and your fellow balloonists commandeer the whole sky, and because of the way sound travels up there, you can converse in a normal voice with people in the other balloons around you. (By the way, if you *are* the skydiving type, hopping out of a hot-air balloon is a singular experience—quite different from jumping out of a plane, I've found. Because there's no airplane noise or commotion, you must leap amid the surrounding stillness and serenity—just the soft *whoosh* of your body going over the side. I found the experience a bit eerie, but memorable.)

Have an animal encounter. This may seem like a thematic departure from the other "leaps" cited, but I think of wildlife encounters as a leap of faith for two reasons: You must be willing to jump down from the safe perch of "civilization" to get on the jungle level of animals, and you must have faith that you can and will come back alive. In my own life, I have come face-to-face with bears, sharks, and various "big cats." On my list of things to do is standing eye-to-eye with an African mountain gorilla (a truly spiritual experience, I'm told). I think my most memorable "wild encounter" was with a whale. I was diving off the coast of Fiji and saw a pod of pilot whales. With my boat's engine turned off, I quietly drifted as close as I could get. Then I softly dove into the water. Within a few moments, I was staring into the gigantic eye of a whale no more than 15 feet away. We stared at each other for what felt like an eternity. Then he disappeared.

Take a dive. Not just into a swimming pool; that's too easy. Cliff diving is a true leap of faith. The bravest (craziest?) cliff divers I've encountered are the "Latin Lemmings," who dive headfirst off the cliffs of Acapulco, 150 feet down into shallow ocean inlets. I wouldn't recommend that, but in Negril, Jamaica, the Pickled Parrot area offers a

(continued)

(continued)

LEAP OF FAITH: POSSIBILITIES

less terrifying cliff dive of 45 feet. And those who are leery of the cliff dive can swing out from a rope and then drop into the water. By the way, be on the lookout for scenic spots closer to home where you can swing on a rope and then dive; it's a very Tarzan-like experience. (Obviously, you should take the plunge only in areas where the water is known to be deep enough for safe diving.) Another possibility I'd recommend is diving down waterfalls, also known as "canyoning." We're not talking about Niagara Falls (for that, you'll need a barrel), but some smaller waterfalls located in canyons are great for diving, as long as they flow into a deep, safe pool underneath. I once dove down a waterfall in New Zealand, headfirst.

Ride the roller coaster. If you're someone who's been on lots of roller coasters, move on to the next item. But if you've always been afraid of them, this could be the challenge for you. It's never too late to learn to love a roller coaster. And besides, do you want to spend the rest of your life apologizing to kids and grandkids who ask you to take them for a ride? But if you're going to make this a unique experience, go all out: I like the idea sent in to N.O.W. by Anthony Mello, whose dream is to ride 72 roller coasters in 72 hours, going from Texas to Cleveland to California and finishing on the High Roller in Las Vegas, the highest coaster in the world. (Mello says that during those 3 days, he would eat only corn dogs and cotton candy; watch out below!)

Jump into a movement. It doesn't matter if it's about cleaning up the environment, cleaning up television, supporting your favorite candidate, increasing cancer awareness, or defending the great mole rat. Whatever the cause may be, joining a movement is a leap of faith because it *demands* that you have faith, and also that you act on it. Like windsurfing, social movements can lift you up and just carry you along on the current, providing a sense of purpose and camaraderie on the way. If you do join a cause, by all means be passionate about it but also try to remain civil; we already have too many people shouting at each other these days.

Fly like Mike. If you want to practice gravity-defying leaps in the comfort of your own backyard, a trampoline is a great investment. Now I'm not recommending you do the following, because I don't want to be held liable for any twisted ankles, but let me tell you what *I* would do if *I* had a trampoline in my yard and a basketball court in my driveway. I would haul that trampoline a few feet in front of the basket, grab hold of a basketball with both hands, and then take a trampoline-propelled leap toward that basket, at which point I would slam-dunk the ball, hang by both hands from the rim for a few seconds shouting, "In your face!" and then let myself drop gently to the ground. But that's just me.

7

REDISCOVER
YOUR CHILDHOOD

WHENEVER ANYONE SAYS, "I'm too old for that," I think of Banana George.

"And who on earth is Banana George?" you may well be asking, which is what I was wondering myself one day 10 years ago, when I was assigned by a television morning show to go interview a man who insisted on referring to himself by this childish name. I was informed that this Banana George fellow was literally making a spectacle of himself down in Winter Haven, Florida. He was performing various hair-raising stunts that would be dangerous for a man in his twenties—and George was pushing 80. Moreover, he was said to be obsessed with the color yellow, and he reportedly consumed mass quantities of bananas. And last but not least, according to eyewitnesses, he could walk on water. At very high speeds. It sounded like a story to me.

When I arrived in Florida, I proceeded to the house of Banana George. His wife, who seemed perfectly normal, greeted me and then introduced me to the man himself. Sure enough, he was dressed in a yellow shirt and yellow trousers. I checked to see if his shoes were yellow and they weren't, but that is only because George doesn't wear shoes. He had white hair that seemed to stand on end as if electrified, a thick white mustache, and bright twinkling eyes. His handshake was a bone-crusher, which should have come as no surprise because it was plain to see he was a solid rock of muscle. George (whose last name is Blair, though he doesn't use it much) immediately treated me like a new best friend. He wanted to show me everything in his house, so he led me from room to room, pointing things out. Every room was yellow. Everything in his clothes closet was yellow. His telephone was yellow and shaped like a banana. He even had a set of yellow drums. As I was admiring them, he leaped behind them, picked up a pair of sticks, and went into a furious solo.

Over the next couple of hours, I got to know a little more about this curious specimen. It seemed as if the clock of George Blair's life had been tinkered with somewhere along the line, at which point it began to run backward. The rewind started about 40 years ago. At the time, George Blair was a fairly typical middle-aged man—he wore a suit every day, ran a successful New Jersey–based business in a decidedly unglamorous field (mosquito fogging equipment), and sometimes complained about his aching back. After undergoing back surgery, he took the advice of his doctor and spent some time recuperating in the warm waters of Florida, watching the water skiers zip by. One day, a water-ski instructor asked him if he wanted to join in the fun. George laughed and said, "Sorry, I'm too old for that." But the instructor wouldn't listen. George agreed to try some lessons. When he did, something clicked, and it wasn't in his back.

From that point on, George got progressively younger. He took up water-skiing with a passion. He gradually began to wear suits less often and practically stopped wearing shoes (he'd never liked them to begin with and had always loved being barefoot). He kept running his business operations, including a bank, in the Northeast but began to free himself up for more and more trips down to Florida. He opened a water-skiing school of his own. And he began paying frequent visits to Cypress Gardens, renowned for its water-skiing shows. It was there that George had another revelation when he saw someone skiing on the water *without skis*. "I was 46 years old the first time I saw someone barefoot water-ski," George told me. "It looked impossible. I knew this was something I had to try."

He was very good at it. So good, in fact, that he was asked to display his "barefooting" skills before the crowds at Cypress Gardens. He had no interest in being paid; he just wanted to show off and have fun. He

How to Give Yourself the Ultimate "Snow Day"

Remember how much fun it was to stay home from school and play in the snow all day? If you're going to create a snow-fun experience, don't settle for drab, grown-up skiing (unless there's a reindeer involved; explanation opposite). The thing to do is get yourself to a true winter wonderland, someplace where you can really rollick in the snow.

I did this a few years ago, on what I called my "Arctic Blast" adventure, which brought me to Finland and Sweden. I sped around on snowmobiles, got into more than a few snowball fights, and then donned an oversized inflated survival suit so that I could float like a human iceberg on the frigid waters. After I'd worn myself out, I spent the night in an ice castle in Kemi, Finland. (There is also an "ice hotel," located in the village of Jukkasjarvi, Sweden, where everything eventually became a featured attraction at Cypress Gardens, where he was known in particular for speeding across the top of the water on the soles of his feet while using his teeth to hang on to a rope that towed him at 37 miles per hour. He also became known for his yellow wetsuit and yellow sunglasses. His love of the color was really nothing new ("I was always attracted to yellow since I was a kid," he says), but now, in his second youth, he felt no need to moderate that passion. He decided to go all yellow, all the time.

As he reached his seventies, George just kept picking up speed. He got himself into the *Guinness Book of Records* in various categories relating to

from the walls to the beds is made fresh each winter from packed snow and ice. Obviously, you need a good blanket, though there are heated cabins if you can't stand the cold. Call 011-46-980-66800 for reservations, and be sure to schedule your trip before May; by then, the ice hotel has melted.)

The highlight of my snow adventure was skiing behind a reindeer. The locals were razzing me, insisting there was no way I could make it through a 1-mile course without falling. Because I was in full kid mode, how could I back down? What I didn't realize was that deer move just as fast when pulling a skier as they do any other time, accelerating from zero to 30 miles per hour in an instant. The course wound through narrow gaps between trees, and all I could do was try to keep my balance and hope the deer didn't lead me astray. I didn't know whether to laugh or scream, so I did both. And when it was all over, I got to relive another classic kid moment: I was awarded my first reindeer driver's license, which I still carry proudly.

barefoot water-skiing. He was doing stunts all over the world by this time: Europe, Russia, Antarctica. He water-skied in India, and a funny thing happened: He let go of the rope on the speeding towboat to see if his momentum would carry him to a nearby shore. A crowd of people saw George coming at them, gliding along the top of the water all by himself, on those remarkable bare feet of his. Some apparently thought they were witnessing a miracle. When George came strolling up on the shore, people rushed up to him. "They wanted to touch me, as if they'd seen Christ walking on the water," he says with bemusement. Sometime after this, David Letterman invited George to be on his television show, wanting to know, among other things, *What is the deal with the yellow?* And shortly after that is when I came calling.

NATURALLY, I WANTED TO SEE a demonstration of George's un-canny skill, and just as naturally, he was eager to oblige. His wife, JoAnne, piloted the yellow speedboat, as she often does for George. My camera-man filmed George as he hammed it up on the water in his yellow wetsuit, hollering and waving madly and doing the rope-in-the-teeth trick. I don't know that I've ever seen a grown man have so much fun. As soon as the cameras were turned off and George pulled himself back on the boat, he said to me, "So, would you like to learn how to barefoot water-ski?"

Within a few minutes, I was the one hanging on to the boom (a pole that sticks out from the side of the boat), and George was in the boat barking instructions at me: *"Back straight." "Bend the knees." "Lean forward."* I was on one ski, with the other foot bare. He had me slowly press down on the water with that bare foot while still riding on the ski. Then he coached me as I gradually tried shifting weight over to the bare foot. For a human to be able to stand on water requires a complex and delicate balancing act— the feet and body must be positioned just so, the boat must be going a precise speed in formulaic relation to the body weight and foot size of the skier, and everything must be exactly right. But somehow George taught me to do this in a span of 45 minutes. I was amazed and ecstatic and, before long, overconfident. I raised a fist and yelled, "George, I'm doing it!" at which time I lost my balance and was face-planted into the water. When I came up for air, George was having a great laugh.

After my assignment was done, I wanted to stay in touch with George. This is quite common among many who encounter him; people who've seen him just once at an exhibition somewhere tend to send notes and birthday wishes to his Web site. I think I know why people are drawn to George: It's because he makes them feel young. Watching him do these amazing things and have so much fun at 80, you feel as if you've got all the time in the world to enjoy life, and that the possibilities are endless. You realize it's never too late to take up water-skiing, or maybe give snowboarding a shot.

Speaking of which, when I found out George was a radically good snowboarder (and why wouldn't he be? He's been doing it ever since he was 75), I arranged, a couple of years after our initial meeting, to go shredding with him. He put me to shame, and after a full day going up and down the mountain, he didn't want to stop; he never wants to stop. After that, we kept meeting up occasionally, every time I needed a youth fix. And then when I had a crazy idea a few years ago to renew my wedding vows underwater, I tried to think of who might serve as an underwater best man (I'd already lined up an underwater priest). I immediately thought of George, and he was of course tickled by the idea—any excuse to do something new and a little crazy is fine by him. George doesn't like to go too deep in the water, so he dropped the rings from a distance—and they gently floated down into my hand. I was waiting in my black scuba gear; the bride wore a white veil. And I don't need to tell you what color George wore.

What Do You Want to Be When You Grow Up?

If you were like a lot of kids, you once wanted to be:

A cowboy

A race car driver

An astronaut

A firefighter

A ballerina or a figure skater

Well, now is the time to become one, and here's how. At the Arizona Cowboy College (www.cowboycollege.com), a 6-day course teaches you how to ride horses and rope steer, in the company of bona fide cowboys. Courses also cover how to run a ranch, how to keep cattle healthy, how to shoe a horse (that's *shoe*, not shoot), and the always popular "branding, ear marking, and tagging."

If you prefer your horses under the hood, the Derek Daly Performance Driving Academy in Las Vegas (www.derekdaley.com) is one of a number of racing schools out there that will teach you everything you need to know to compete in NASCAR (in theory). The school

I KNOW IT'S UNLIKELY that you or I will be water-skiing when we're 89 years old (that's George's current age, and when I checked in with him as this book went to press, sure enough, he was headed for a water-skiing event in France). Very few people have been blessed with a body that will hold up that long and that well. But all of us, I believe, have some of George's childlike spirit inside us. That kid within you is uses specially designed Formula 2000 race cars that are, according to Derek, "very, very fast."

Meanwhile, at the Adult Space Academy in Alabama (www2. spacecamp.com), you'll learn what 4 Gs feels like as you're shot into the air, you'll experience weightlessness, and you'll get to land a space shuttle. Tours of NASA's Marshall Space Flight Center and the U.S. Space and Rocket Center are also included.

To get a taste of firefighting, you don't even have to go to school. Just sign up for the auxiliary firefighter brigade in your own city or town. Not only do you get to live out a childhood fantasy, you contribute a valuable bit of community service in the process.

Finally, it's never too late to master that double axel. Even if you haven't figure skated since childhood, it's easy to glide back into the sport via group lessons offered at many local rinks. The U.S. Figure Skating Association (www.usfsa.org) oversees a "learn to skate" program that encompasses more than 800 programs and 100,000 skaters registered across the country. Also known as the "Basic Skills Program," it's where you learn the fundamentals of figure skating. Once you've mastered those, you're eligible to join a local skating club. Next step after that . . . the Olympics.

just waiting for the chance to emerge, the way Banana George emerged (rip-roaring at 37 miles per hour) from the middle-aged George Blair.

But for this to happen, you, the adult, must do your part. Psychologists will tell you that you must "come to terms with" or "confront" or perhaps "hug" your so-called "inner child." Actually, I think all you need to do is let the poor kid out every once in a while to run around and have some fun.

And if there's one thing that inner kid knows how to do, it's have fun. Children are better than adults when it comes to playing. And laughing. And learning. And exploring. In a lot of ways, they're better than us at *experiencing*, in general. Nature designed them to be alert, curious, imaginative, adaptable. In other words, children just happen to have a lot of the skills *you're* going to need as you pursue all the challenges on your List for Life. With that in mind, I think that "Rediscover Your Childhood" is an important theme that should be addressed on your list. It's a way to inject some playful fun, but there's another benefit, too: If you can find a way to let that inner kid free, he or she can probably help you to do a lot of other things on your list, too.

Of course, if you really want to get more in touch with your childlike qualities, you may want to approach this more as an ongoing process than as a single experience. After all, you don't want to let that kid out just one time and then lock him away again. The idea is to gradually reconnect with a more youthful attitude and spirit and then have these things remain a part of your life. The experience written on your N.O.W. list may be an ultimate expression of that spirit—a particularly glorious day in the sun for the kid within—but it should not be an isolated instance.

THE TOP-SECRET FORMULA FOR YOUTH

So how do you begin this process? Well, of course, everyone claims to have a formula for helping you feel younger: a wonder pill, a vitamin supplement, a surgical procedure. I don't know if there's anything you can ingest that will do the trick (though George prescribes a lot of water and bananas). I think the key to rediscovering your childhood has more to do with *attitude* and *imagination* than anything else.

Start with attitude: One of the biggest problems that we adults have— and this can be a huge obstacle when it comes to trying to live in a *No Opportunity Wasted* way—is that we tend to be jaded. We've seen it all be-

BANANA GEORGE'S TIPS FOR STAYING YOUNG

George, who will turn 90 in early 2005, recommends the following:

Drink plenty of water. He drinks 8 glasses a day. Not counting what he swallows if he happens to fall while barefoot water-skiing.

Eat mostly vegetables and fish.

And a lot of bananas. George has been known to go through 2 tons of bananas a year (he does give some away).

Exercise. When not water-skiing, "I run up and down stairs in my house four or five times a day," he says. "I start slow and build."

Do what you love. "That's what keeps me excited."

Keep trying new things. George took up snowboarding at 75, drove a race car for the first time at 80, and rode his first bull at 84. Recently, he rode his first Segway.

Take off your shoes whenever possible. "God made the human foot so we could go barefoot."

Think young. "I hang out with people half my age. No, make that one-third my age."

Think yellow. "I believe in that color—it's happy, engaging, inspirational, and very bright."

fore. We've heard the sales pitch too many times (and frankly, we're just not buying). We've tried this or that already and it didn't work. Or if we didn't try it ourselves, we know someone who tried it, and it wasn't all it was cracked up to be. Been there, done that.

Kids don't bring this kind of baggage to their life experiences. They're wide-open. They look around and see fresh opportunities everywhere. They're constantly surprised. Some of this is just a matter of inexperi-

UP A TREE

When I was a kid, I used to build tree huts and then sleep in them. There's something glorious about waking up in a tree: the morning sun streaming through the leaves, the birds warbling their first songs on the branch beside you. I hadn't experienced that for quite a while, until a recent trip to Costa Rica. I let it be known that I was looking for a good tree to sleep in and was informed that I'd better pick a tall one. There are lots of snakes in Costa Rica, and if you're anywhere near the ground, you're on their turf. Fortunately, I located an outfitter who had created a network of trees interconnected by cables, about 100 feet above the ground. You hook up and then slide along on the cable from one tree to the next—it's a system Tarzan would have loved, much easier than swinging on vines. On several of these trees, platforms had been constructed that were just about big enough for a person to lie down on. I'm not one of those people who needs a gigantic bed, but this was really tight. If you rolled over just once, you were going to fall out of bed, and that's a big deal when your bed's 100 feet high.

So I lay stiff as a mummy on my little plank, the rain tapping on the

ence (everything really *is* new to them, so of course they find it more interesting), but some of it is attitude and perspective. It's how you choose to view the world, and how you react to it. The writer Franz Kafka said, *"Youth is happy because it has the ability to see beauty. Anyone who keeps the ability to see beauty never grows old."* But how do you keep seeing beauty? It may sound obvious, but the only way is to open your eyes—*wide*. Look hard, and long. Artists and writers have sometimes spoken of trying to

tarp stretched out above me. The experience brought me right back to childhood—the fun of being alone in the dark outdoors, in a secret little place where anything might happen. I got some sleep eventually but was awake by sunup, when I was serenaded by the cacophony of sounds of a jungle morning. Those noises you hear coming from the trees? They're a lot louder when you're *in* the tree. But I loved listening to them, trying to distinguish one call from another. I noticed one that sounded like a whirring noise—and it seemed to be drawing closer. I turned toward it and saw a species I had never observed before: It was the flying Costa Rican coffee man. He was traveling toward me at a good 20 miles an hour on the cable, a cup cradled in each hand. I made room for him on the little platform, and we sat together and sipped, enjoying a view you just won't find at Starbucks.

If you're interested in climbing your own tree, check out www.treeclimbing.com, the site for Tree Climbers International. They offer courses that will teach you how to get to the top of a 300-foot redwood using various forms of climbing gear. At the top, you can hang your own hammock. Which, come to mention it, sounds a lot more comfortable than a tiny platform.

see the world through a child's eyes, which really means looking closer at things, studying and admiring the details, as if you're seeing something for the first time. This is a great exercise for all adults, not just artists. Try looking at your own backyard that way, and you'll notice things you never saw before.

THE OPEN-DOOR POLICY

Of course, opening your eyes doesn't do much good unless you open the doors in your mind, as well. This is really the crux of the matter when it comes to youthful attitude: whether you are willing to let new things in, or whether you bar that door and say, "No thanks, got enough, don't need any more." If you're reading this book and even considering creating a List for Life, then you're probably not someone who bars the door to new experiences altogether. But you may not be opening that door often enough, or wide enough. Many people tend to close themselves off from new experiences slowly and continually as they grow older. And then there's someone like George, whose doors remain wide-open at 89. The good news for all of us is that door hinges don't just move in one direction. Even if they've been swinging closed for a while, they can start swinging back open tomorrow. It's really up to us: *Openness is an attitude.* It can suddenly emerge in people who previously didn't seem particularly open. In the end, it is a choice—or rather, a lot of choices, countless little yes-or-no decisions that you make each time you encounter an opportunity or potential experience.

Of course, it's not enough to crack your door open and then wait passively for opportunities to come to you. Having a youthful attitude means you're also willing to venture out and pursue those possibilities.

Kids will charge headlong out into the world every chance they get. They're not afraid of getting dirty. They're not scared of looking foolish. And they're not worried about all the things they don't know—they figure what they don't know, they'll learn.

Adults, on the other hand, tend to be leery of learning. We're all too aware of the saying about old dogs and new tricks, and a lot of us believe it deep down inside. We may think it's too late for us to constantly absorb new skills the way a sponge-like kid does. But the main reason kids are so good at learning is because they don't think or worry or obsess, they just go ahead and *do*. Whether it's swinging a golf club or fooling around on a computer, they'll tinker and try everything until they get it right. As it happens, in the career I've chosen (which often involves throwing myself into strange situations and then trying to figure out what to do next), I have had to constantly learn new skills on the fly. And I've found the best way to learn as an adult is to take a childlike attitude, as in, "Who cares if I get it right the first time. Let's just give it a go and see what happens."

IMAGINATION
IS YOUR CURRENCY

If you really want to tap into your own kid powers, the right attitude will take you a big part of the way. But you'll need imagination to take you the rest of the way. It is the secret weapon of children, the tool that enables them to create N.O.W. moments out of almost nothing. Think about it: A child can transform a mundane afternoon in the backyard into a thoroughly absorbing, engaging, otherworldly experience—all by the power of imagination. As adults, we're fortunate enough to have the

REUNITING THE
OLD SCHOOLYARD GANG

Ever wonder what became of the friends you grew up with? Ever think about bringing that old gang together to relive a childhood experience? Dan Klores thought about it and then decided to do something about it. The result was a N.O.W. moment, captured brilliantly on film.

It all started a few years ago when Klores, a middle-aged, successful New York public relations executive, had a brief brush with death because of a serious illness. That got him thinking about both his future and his past. Klores had grown up playing basketball on a beloved outdoor court near Brooklyn's Coney Island, surrounded by a group of boys who became very close—and later drifted apart. Some 40 years later, Klores felt the urge to reconnect with those old friends and bring them back to that court on 2nd Street for one more game. And he wanted to film the whole experience.

Klores had never made a full-length film before. Neither had his old friend, ad executive Ron Berger, who agreed to help Klores produce the documentary. "At first, we assumed we'd need to hire a professional film director, and we spent a lot of time looking for one," Klores says. "Then someone said, 'Why don't you just do it yourselves?' and we did."

resources and mobility to move beyond the backyard, but we still need imagination to help us dream of where to go, how to get there, and how to make it all as extraordinary as possible. We're capable of employing imagination almost as well as a child does, though in our case a bit of stretching and warming up may be required; there could be flabbiness from lack of use. Don't go to a gym for this exercise. Just find a quiet

Learning to become a film director was only part of the challenge. Tracking down those far-flung childhood pals was even harder. It brought surprises for Klores, not all of them pleasant. One old friend had drifted into homelessness; another had been murdered; another had lost a child. All of those harrowing stories became part of the film. But the various twists of fate hadn't changed one thing: The boys of 2nd Street Park still felt a strong bond with one another. And many of them agreed to return to the park for a reunion game.

Klores himself laced up his sneakers and played, as did Berger (with a cameraman filming the whole time). "It was thrilling to be playing with the guys again after all those years," Klores says. Afterward, one of the other players told him, "As soon as I stepped onto that court, I was 15 all over again."

That feeling in itself made the whole effort worthwhile, says Klores. But there was another reward still to come: The film that he and Berger finished making, "The Boys of 2nd Street Park," received a standing ovation at the Sundance Film Festival and then aired on the Showtime cable channel (it's now available on DVD). All of which has launched a second career for the rejuvenated Klores, who is now putting the finishing touches on his second documentary film.

little room downstairs, or a spot in a distant corner of the yard, or, best of all, a tree house.

Once you've extracted yourself from the "adult" world of everyday realities and distractions, you're ready to begin that journey back to childhood. Think about what you loved to do when you were a kid; re-create in your head one of the best kid days you ever had. But also let yourself dream about what you could do now, what you'd truly love to do, and what you're going to do. Think small (childish) and big (ambitious) at the same time. Let your imagination roam without restraint, but as you do, keep a notepad and pen—or crayon—close at hand. Because these are not just idle backyard fantasies you're dreaming up; each of these

A Day in the Life of a Child

Maybe it was the first day you had a picnic at the beach. Or the time you went sledding all day long and came home to some steaming hot chocolate. Everyone has memories of a great day from childhood. But what would it be like if you tried to relive that day? It's a fun exercise to try—and a good way to begin the process of rediscovering your childhood. Take the following three steps back in time.

1. Re-create the day in your mind and write down the details: What did you do, who was there, what made it special? The little things are important: Do you remember what you were wearing? And what color your sneakers were? What kind of soda did you drink?

2. Try to set up a return engagement, if possible, in the same place, with as many of the same people as you can gather. Go out of your way to get some of the same things you had then: the same potato chips, the same type of football. These things mattered to you when you were a kid; if you're going to go back, they have to matter again.

3. When it's time to relive that day, do everything the way you would have done it as a kid. Don't be afraid to yell. Or to tease

ideas represents an opportunity to start living with a more youthful attitude. Each one is a chance to open the door a little wider and let that kid inside come running out. So write all of these childish ideas down on your notepad, but take the very best of the batch and write it on your List for Life.

your pals the way you used to. Burp if you like. Most of all, cut loose and have fun.

The day I remember best from my own childhood happened when I was 11 years old. I was living on the island of Antigua at the time. My father had gotten a job there. We lived modestly, as did most people on the island: no television, no fresh milk. But I had one very important possession and that was my bike. I used to ride it all across the island, getting to know every nook and cranny. Sometimes the local adult bike riders on the island would let me tag along with them, this one little white kid peddling furiously to keep up. One day, I got a crazy idea in my head, the way kids do. I decided to organize a bike-a-thon to raise money for these local cyclists and their club. I rode around in advance getting people to sponsor me by the mile—the goal was to ride 50 miles, much farther than I'd ever gone. The day of the bike-a-thon, I felt like a local celebrity: The older bikers joined me on the ride and cheered me on, and my dad took photos at stops along the way. When I completed the 50-mile ride, I felt like it was the biggest thing I'd ever done in my life (which it probably was). That's the day that lives in my mind. And I do plan to go back to Antigua sometime, take that same ride, round up some of the same riders if I can find them. And have my dad take pictures along the way.

REDISCOVER YOUR CHILDHOOD: POSSIBILITIES

When it comes to childish possibilities, there are almost too many to choose from. If you're looking for some little starters—things that are easy to do and will begin to get you in the right frame of mind—flying a kite is an old standby. The same can be said of board games, particularly old favorites from childhood like Scrabble and Monopoly. Pictionary is great because it forces you to draw, often with hilarious results. To boost the "experience quotient" on game playing, take the games outdoors to a park and arrange an all-day high-stakes tournament; put kids in charge as referees. These are just warmups to more elaborate possibilities such as:

Play it again. This has proven to be a big theme among people writing in to the N.O.W. television series. The idea is to go back and re-play a big sports game from childhood. If you're going to do this right, you need to go all out and do a lot of pregame coordination. Assemble all the players from both teams in a Little League or high school game, even including cheerleaders if there were any. It works best with two teams that had a special rivalry: Maybe they played in the league championship, or maybe they competed in terms of last-place ineptitude (that's even more fun). And there are nonsports possibilities, too: You can restage a school play with all the same actors.

Go treasure hunting. It's every kid's fantasy to go diving for buried treasure. And it's all around. You can start on land with a metal detector, combing the beaches. But the good stuff is under the sea. Almost any scuba-diving experience brings the sensation of discovery, the feeling that you're seeing life forms and rocks that no one else gets to see. You may be lucky enough to find some pirate booty down there, but you'll increase your odds considerably if you join up with a salvage operation that specializes in shipwreck dives.

Stay up all night. I'm a big believer in "up-all-night marathons"—seeing how far you can prolong an experience, going past the point of fatigue. We've all had that childhood thrill of staying up late and breaking the rules, even as an adult. I did it once in New York City, completing a full 28-hour stretch of tourism from dawn to dawn, with my cameraman Scott filming the whole time (I don't know how his shoulder held up). The best part was the wee hours of the morning, when it's just you and the die-hard night creatures. By 4:00 in the morning, my eyes were bleary, but I have a hazy memory of a deserted all-night bar where someone did a dance involving cellophane.

Get dirty! This is one of the true pleasures of being a kid: You can make a mess of yourself and enjoy doing it. You don't have to search far for "dirty" opportunities; the mud in the yard is a good starting point. But if you want to go all out, I'll suggest two of the messiest possibilities in the world. The first is La Tomatina, which has been called the ultimate food fight. It takes place each summer in Bunol, Spain. The action begins when a firecracker explodes: That's the signal for everyone to begin throwing tomatoes at one another. By the time it's over, more than 40 tons of tomatoes will have been splattered and you will, without a doubt, be seeing red. (For more information, visit the Tourist Office of Spain's Web site, www.tourspain.es.) And when it's time to wash off after La Tomatina, you can hop over to Wales to take part in a "bog snorkeling" competition, which has established itself as "the world's yuckiest race" (that is an official title, by the way).

Get back on that bike. If you think back on your childhood, you'll probably recall that some of your best experiences happened on a bicycle. If you've stopped riding a bike, you absolutely must climb back into the saddle seat, immediately. Start slow with rides around the local park to get your legs back. Then get started on planning an odyssey. A week on a bike can take you through an entire country, and you'll see it close-up, in a way you never could by car or train. One of my favorites:

(continued)

(continued)

REDISCOVER YOUR CHILDHOOD:
POSSIBILITIES

Bike the wine trail in Napa Valley (but make sure you drink more water than wine lest you swerve off the trail). Bike trips are also great for bonding with your kids or with old friends, or even new ones.

Take lessons—and pay attention this time. Remember those piano lessons or ballet classes you were forced to take as a kid? Go back and retake them, but this time do it with a passion. Some of the things you didn't fully appreciate as a kid take on a whole new dimension when you do them as an adult (especially since *you're* paying for them now). And taking adult lessons is a great way to remind yourself that it's never too late to learn. Jeff Goodby, who runs one of the world's most successful ad agencies, Goodby, Silverstein & Partners, recently began taking violin lessons—at age 52. Another acquaintance of mine took up horseback riding, something she'd tried and never mastered as a kid. If you're learning a new skill as an adult, give yourself time to have fun and make mistakes. But also give yourself a goal and maybe even a N.O.W. challenge to shoot for down the line: a public performance in front of friends and relatives, a recital, a steeple jump.

Get scared. Only children seem to appreciate what a wonderfully cathartic experience it is to scare the heck out of yourself. I'm not talking "bungee scared" here so much as "monster scared." This is another great experience to share with your kids: Turn your home-sweet-home into a house of horrors (just temporarily, mind you). If you don't know how to do that, ask the kids—they'll have plenty of suggestions. If you don't want to mess with your own house, find the nearest haunted house that will let you spend the night. While there, swap ghost stories with your companions. If you're willing to go a long way for chills and thrills, think about spending dark nights in Dracula's castle. That's right, we mean the Count himself, also known as Vlad the Impaler. His Transylvania castle is now open to the public, and a trip there includes visits to his grave and spooky séances (for more information, visit Quest Tours at www.romtour.com).

Get rolling. Like cycling, inline skating can take you back to childhood memories. But its advantage over cycling is that it can be a very social activity, allowing you to become part of a rolling community and special event. A lot of cities have Friday Night Skate Nights that turn this childlike activity into a kind of performing art form for the masses (the Friday night ritual in Paris draws up to 25,000 skaters). If you really want to shoot for a N.O.W. event, you can organize some type of coordinated skate performance in your community.

Get in the "Zorb." Maybe it's just me, but I think this is another great New Zealand invention that is destined to be as big as bungee. A Zorb is a giant beach ball that you climb inside; it has two layers, and trapped within the outer layer are soapsuds. In the center of it all is you, trying to stand up and walk as the ball rolls down a hill. It has been compared with being inside a tumbling clothes dryer, but that doesn't do the experience justice. All I can say is that I never feel more like a child than when I am rolling around inside the Zorb (check out www.zorb.com for more information).

I have a lot of miscellaneous childish things on my own list. I can't explain why I want to do these things, but hey—when you're a kid, you don't have to explain. That said, I would like to:

- Putt a golf ball coast to coast across Scotland.
- Be a ball boy for a day at the U.S. Open.
- Enter and win a hot dog eating competition.
- Wear a full-body Velcro suit and throw myself against a wall.
- Spend 3 days on the Bahamian Bruise Cruise with pro wrestlers.

8

SHED YOUR INHIBITIONS/ EXPRESS YOURSELF

PICTURE THIS: The scene is downtown Los Angeles, or to be more exact, Cantor's Kosher Deli. With the spicy aroma of pastrami wafting through the air, men munch on thick meat sandwiches while an old woman ladles her soup; the middle-aged waiters are efficient and brusque. Sitting in a booth with his back turned on the outside world, Etan Goldman does not realize that I am creeping up from behind, a television camera crew in tow. I want to surprise him. I want spontaneity, and I want drama. I want some pastrami, too, but that can wait.

When I'm almost on top of him, I call out his name. He turns around in shock, and I ask him the familiar question: *"Etan, are you ready to do your dream?"* He's ready—boy, is he ready. He is so excited he stands up on his chair right there in the middle of the deli and announces to everyone in the room, "Starting now, I'm going to prove to the world that I can be . . . *a Jewish rapper."*

The surrounding deli customers are silent for a beat—stunned, no doubt. Then it begins, slowly at first, but building: the laughter. Yes, they all guffaw, and it doesn't seem to surprise Etan, who just nods his head and smiles. "It's what I'm used to," he says, glancing down at me. "Everybody laughs when I tell them this."

I'd received Etan's letter to *No Opportunity Wasted* earlier. It got right to the point: "I am a Jewish rapper," he explained, "and my mom doesn't really 'get' the career path I've chosen for myself. My dream is to make a music video of one of my songs and have my mom come out and watch how hard I work to do what I do." I was immediately drawn to the story and its timeless theme: For as long as artists have been expressing themselves, they've had to contend with the oppressive forces of government censorship, as well as the cold realities of a brutal commercial marketplace. But all of that's nothing compared with a disapproving mother. On top of that, as Etan explained in his letter, "my mother-in-law isn't too thrilled with what I do either."

Still, this hadn't discouraged Etan. The idea of becoming a musician was no idle fantasy for him. At age 37, he'd drifted in and out of several dozen jobs (much to the dismay of his mother). He couldn't seem to work up a passion for anything other than his music. He saw it as a means of opening up and sharing a part of himself—in particular, he wanted to convey his perspective as an Orthodox Jew, in hopes of forging a connection between that world and the world of the street. Etan felt that his music could break down cultural barriers. And he had no doubt that he could impress a prestigious hip-hop producer and gain acceptance among hard-core rap audiences. Whether he could win over his mom was another matter.

With a little push from N.O.W., Etan began lining up a whirlwind series of preliminary meetings with producers, while simultaneously putting together a music video. He flew his mother in from New York City, though she did not know why. When the moment of truth arrived, Etan stood prepared to bare his talents before two very tough judges: a hotshot producer named Raj, who was wearing a glittering gold chain and medallion, and Etan's mother, who wore a smaller, simpler necklace. Etan pushed "play" and the music video started. What followed was a 3-minute rap that was religious, rebellious, and, above all, righteous. When it was over, Etan looked to the producer first. "I think there's a place for this in the market," Raj said. Then Etan looked at his mother. She was shaking her head, but only a little, and that was a good sign.

RAJ DID SIGN ETAN TO A CONTRACT, and it looks like there's a record deal in the works—which may or may not make Etan's mother happy. But the way I see it, Etan won the battle just by being willing to stand and deliver before an audience that might easily have dismissed him (or sent him to his room). Although there may not be an abundance of Orthodox Jewish rappers out there, I think Etan's situation is universal in a way. He had something deep inside that he wanted and needed to express, but he felt inhibited by the attitudes and expectations of people around him—in particular, his mother. Etan's story brings together two related themes that are merged in this chapter: the need in all of us to express ourselves freely, and the realization that, to do so, we must often shake off some of the inhibitions that hold us back.

I believe that finding ways to express yourself creatively and passion-ately can be as exhilarating and freeing as any physical adventure you can have. Obviously, we all express ourselves every day in routine, ordinary ways: the "Hi, how are you?" of normal conversation, the e-mails and memos we write, the choice of a colorful necktie or scarf to wear to the office. But what we hold back is often the good stuff: the heartfelt mes-sage we'd love to shout out to the world, the vision we feel compelled to paint or carve or film or paste together, the desire to strut and flaunt, perhaps in outrageous attire (or maybe in no attire at all). In everyone, I believe, there's *something* in there, some kind of deep personal statement, that wants and needs to come out. And the key to turning this need into a full-fledged N.O.W. experience—number 6 on your List for Life—is to figure out what that something is and then find a bold, memorable, *ultimate* means of expressing it to the world.

To do this, however, requires not just creative soul-searching but something more: a willingness to push through the walls that have confined and trapped this particular something inside you for so long. Those walls are your inhibitions. We all have them, and they can serve a useful purpose at times. When you're in a sour mood and feel the sudden urge to tell your boss what you *really* think of his management style, inhibition is what makes you bite your tongue and avoid career suicide. But if that same suppression mechanism keeps you from expressing *anything* to your boss, then it becomes a counterproductive force in your career. Moreover, inhibitions can extend into almost all aspects of your life, particularly social situations. They can keep you from reaching out to others, or from baring your own soul and personality to those around you. And in so doing, they can cause you to miss out on experiences and opportunities that could enrich your life.

In chapter 3, we looked at the way fears can place restrictions and limits on your life, and the same is true with inhibitions. That's not surprising, because inhibitions are, of course, intertwined with and driven by fear. But often, they seem to be most connected to one narrow and very specific fear: "If I do X, Y, or Z, what will other people think? Will I embarrass myself?"

On the surface, fear of embarrassment or disapproval may seem less gripping than the mortal fear of a shark bite or a fall from 200 feet up. Yet inhibitions can be just as paralyzing as these more "extreme" fears. And they're likely to affect you much more often, having a larger impact on your life. Inhibitions based on fear of embarrassment or disapproval can keep you from "shining"—from showing your true talents and living up to your potential. They can keep you from growing. They can even keep you from just being yourself.

So shed 'em, I say. Of course, I do realize that shedding your inhibitions is not as easy as peeling off an extra layer of clothing on a warm day. But

TEST YOUR IQ

Take the following quiz to test your "Inhibition Quotient." Answer True or False. Give yourself 20 points for each time you answer "False."

1. I have made at least five new friends in the past 3 years. T/F

2. I have gone skinny-dipping at least once in my life. T/F

3. When someone needs to stand up and give a toast at a family function, I'm always willing to do it. T/F

4. When I walk into a room full of strangers, I'll generally say hello to someone right away. T/F

5. I always liked wearing outrageous costumes to Halloween parties. T/F

6. I have gone under the limbo stick at least three times in my life. T/F

7. I often burst out in song (and not just in the shower). T/F

8. When I'm in a group and something good happens, I'll yell, "Yee-haw!" T/F

Results: If your Inhibition Quotient is 160, you are a genius when it comes to carefully constructing walls around yourself. All you need now is a sledgehammer. If your IQ is 120, you are as smart as a computer geek when it comes to socializing. If your IQ is 80, you are normal, which means like most people, you're pretty stiff but you have your moments. An IQ of 40 means your inhibitions are low, which is why you're able to leap over them most of the time; good for you. If your IQ is 0, then you have no inhibitions and might want to think about developing just a few.

in a funny way, that analogy of shedding clothes is an apt one—because ultimately, in both cases, exposure is the desired result. And whether you're exposing your body, your true feelings, or your talent, the risk is the same: the possibility of embarrassment and the chance that someone may disapprove. The trick is to come to understand that those are rather small, inconsequential risks. The embarrassment may not happen at all, and if it does, it will probably be only momentary. It's certainly a chance worth taking. And the good news is, you can begin shedding inhibitions gradually, exposing yourself a little bit at a time. You don't have to go buck-naked all at once. Unless your quest to shed inhibitions happens to take you to a Palm Springs nudist resort, which is where, a few years ago, I decided to give my own inhibitions the heave-ho.

NUDE AWAKENING

The experience was a real eye-opener for me in more ways than one. I went as a guest of a nude wedding, not really sure if I was going to partake in the full Monty or just remain a clothed bystander. My first day at the resort, I was the only one in clothes (oddly, when you're the sole person in a room who's dressed, you feel more exposed than the people who actually are exposed). I suppose "revelations" are pretty common at a nudist camp, but I had one that surprised me: This group of people seemed totally relaxed around each other, accepting, and able to make friends easily. It was as if, by getting rid of that layer of clothes, they also removed social barriers. As one of the "naturists" explained to me, when you socialize among people without clothes, you have no way of knowing if the person you're talking to is a stylish snob or just a poor slob. Everybody is equal (give or take an inch here or there). And so everybody seems more willing to approach one another with an open mind.

SHOWING YOUR "HELL'S ANGEL" SIDE

Suppose you're in your forties, a respectable suburban mother of two, and you work in an anesthesiology lab by day. Does this mean you can't wear a leather jacket and roar around on a motorcycle? Not according to Barb Hammond of Tecumseh, Michigan, who shared her inspiring story with *No Opportunity Wasted*.

"I am a 48-year-old mother of two wonderful daughters. Like most parents, I was always there for them when they were young children, which really cut out my social life. After healing from a painful divorce, I decided I wanted to pursue my dream—to start riding a motorcycle again. This was a dream I had planned with my ex-husband; I decided I was not going to let the dream die just because the marriage did. I started saving the money. I am not sure what flipped the switch, but one weekend I was compelled to go out to look at motorcycles. By the end of the day, I had placed a down payment on a used Suzuki, with 2 days to think about it.

"I talked it over with friends. At first, they were shocked that I was doing this. They didn't really try to talk me out of it, but they did play the 'injury, dismemberment, and death' card a lot. My daughters were especially worried—lots of conversations about not wanting to lose me to an accident. (That changed over time; they are actually proud of me riding a motorcycle now, and they love it when their friends comment on what a 'cool' mom they have.)

This was an epiphany that made perfect sense to me—yet I still clung to my own little barrier, a pair of swim trunks, well into my second day

"I was scared to death when I took possession of the motorcycle. It actually sat in the garage for a week or so, and I would look at it thinking, 'What did I just do?' I had to force myself to take it out. But I found that once I was out on the road, I was free of all the day's worries. It wasn't long before the apprehension was gone. I even forced myself to learn about the engine so that I could do my own maintenance.

"I gradually made some new 'riding' friends as I eased back onto the roads. My dream achieved its highest level last August when I rode my bike with these new friends, traveling all the way from eastern Michigan to Milwaukee for the Harley-Davidson 100th birthday celebration. I have to admit, I was not sure what I was getting into by riding a bike that far—I just knew I wanted to do it, come what may. The feeling of freedom on that ride was amazing. And talk about 'shedding inhibitions.' When I am in my leather chaps and vest and do-rag, I look nothing like my day-to-day self. It is almost like I am in an 'alter-ego' mode—a little more rowdy and adventurous, kind of larger than life. When we got to the Harley event, it was perfect; unless you were there, it is hard to convey the sights, sounds, and hospitality we were shown the entire time.

"The return trip brought cold steady rain as our companion for the 10-hour ride back to Michigan. But we found solace in the many other riders sharing the road home. Vehicle traffic was very courteous with us. Bless them all. Looking back, I will never forget any of the trip: my new friends, wonderful memories, and the pride that I took that first step to get back on a bike. Looking forward, I hope for more trips, more friends, and if I am lucky, maybe a new Harley Softail. The dream continues."

there. It wasn't until the actual wedding (the bride wore a veil, the groom a bow tie, and that was all, folks) that I finally did drop trou, because, after all, it wouldn't be proper to wear swim trunks to a wedding. Having exposed myself, I soon discovered that I was the only one who cared deeply about this occurrence. To everyone else, I was just another naked body, albeit a welcome one in this group. I think there's a lesson here for would-be shedders of all sorts of inhibitions: Don't assume other people will judge you harshly. If they've ever known what it's like to bare their own butts, they'll probably look gently upon yours.

Going naked may be the most literal means of self-exposure, but it's just one of many ways to "let it all hang out." You can also go in the opposite

PASSING THE RED HAT

If you've recently encountered a group of women wearing red hats with purple dresses and having a rollicking good time, you've just crossed paths with a chapter of the Red Hat Society (www.redhatsociety .com). The group has registered more than 25,000 chapters (an estimated 600,000 members worldwide) and has become a social phenomenon that is now being studied by doctors, sociologists, and grad students trying to gauge and comprehend the group's apparently enormous impact on the lives of women over the age of 50.

It all started about 5 years ago when group founder Sue Ellen Cooper bought a bright red fedora at a thrift shop. Sometime after that, Cooper came upon a line in a poem: "When I am an old woman I shall wear purple with a red hat which doesn't go. . . ." She started giving red hats and copies of the poem to her friends, and they did likewise. Soon they had formed a small Red Hat Society and could be seen around California going out for tea in the red hats and purple dresses and referring to one another by their self-chosen titles ("Exalted Queen Mother," "Princess Daughter," "Sergeant in direction—*putting on* clothes to make a statement. If you're someone who has always dressed conservatively or plainly, this can be a fun way of challenging your own inhibitions. If you're not ready to go head-to-toe "Banana George yellow" just yet, you can start with an attention-grabbing accessory—be it a Three Stooges tie or a funny red hat.

Wearing a funny hat can be an interesting experience, I've learned. I once wore one made of beer cans as I marched in the Mardi Gras in Sydney, Australia, and I noticed a few looks coming my way—though it's possible they were really looking at my Astroturf miniskirted dress. This

Gloves"). From there, it became a movement that swept through California and around the country, then on to Canada, Europe, and Australia.

By dressing gaudily, the women in the group not only have a chance to shed their inhibitions, they also get to make a statement: Just because we're over 50 doesn't mean we can't go a little wild if we so desire. "And even though it starts with just the clothes, it often carries over into a whole attitude," says Cooper. "The idea seems to be, 'Since I'm having fun with the way I dress, then maybe I can also have fun in lots of other ways, too.' " Indeed, Red Hatters have been known to sail the high seas, jump out of airplanes, and go on motorcycle rides. And all of this has raised the spirits and the activity levels of older women who might otherwise be sedentary—which is why some physicians are prescribing the Red Hat Society to patients to improve their physical and mental health. Cooper (who still holds the title of Exalted Queen Mother) reports, "We get e-mails every day from women who say that adding Red Hat Society membership to their lives has been like finding an oasis in the desert of life. The quality of sisterhood that has developed is amazing."

was my one and only cross-dressing adventure (honest!), which came about when the officially designated drag queen of the festival invited me along and even helped dress me for the occasion (my favorite part of the outfit was the butch combat boots, which seemed to complement the turf dress and the beer-can hat). I went out on the town that night, dressed to kill or at least wound. And what I loved about it was that I felt completely immersed in another world. To everyone around me, I *was* a drag queen that night, and they related to me on that level. It was like going undercover and getting an inside look at a world from which I would normally be excluded.

This, I think, cuts to an important point about shedding your inhibitions: doing so can broaden your world. Those inhibiting walls you've built up are keeping unusual things out, and thereby enclosing you in a life of sameness. If you want to be exposed to rich diversity, you must be willing to . . . expose yourself. There's no way around it: To understand the nudist experience, you've got to feel the breeze on your behind. To understand life in drag, you've got to put on the dress. Otherwise, you remain an outside observer, watching from the sidelines in your plain khakis. I'd rather be inside, soaking up some of the life experiences of people who are very different from myself. I like to think that if you do this, you can become more appreciative of diversity, and a more tolerant individual. But at the very least, you'll end up with a damn good story to tell (and maybe even embarrassing pictures).

LETTING DOWN YOUR GUARD

This idea of immersion, a theme also covered in chapter 4, is an important one with regard to shedding inhibitions. The concept is to insert yourself into the mix, to let down your guard and open yourself up to new people and experiences. This doesn't have to involve nudist resorts or drag parades; it can take place at a local pub. I've always maintained that when you're traveling anywhere, you should go where the locals go to drink, even if that place is less than fancy (your inhibitions will try to steer you to the upscale touristy hotel bar, but just keep walking). When you get to this lively dive, plant yourself at the bar and start a conversation with whoever's near you. If you need a drop of social lubricant to grease the wheels, so be it. Order what the locals drink; even if it's some bizarre fermented juice, give it a shot. And if you survive the first one, give it another shot. Soon you just might be joining arms on all sides and singing local folk songs without a clue of the lyrics. You may end up dancing on a table, and that's all right, too (make sure the table legs are sturdy). In Turkey once, I imbibed several shots of something that was sweet and powerful. This not only lowered my inhibitions but obliterated them to such an extent that I agreed to try belly dancing. I think it was a hell of a lot of fun, though I'm not sure. But that night will always be a fond hazy memory.

The great thing about cutting loose when you're in a strange place is that you have nothing to lose. Nobody knows you there, and you'll probably never see those people again. So it's a good opportunity to start chipping away at your inhibitions. Then you can gradually continue the process when you're on your own turf. Because, really, you should be doing the same thing in your hometown—immersing yourself in interesting local gatherings and reaching out to strangers. For many of us, this kind of socializing stops cold at a certain point in adulthood, when we suddenly begin to circle the wagons and cease making friends. And before long, we're living a life in which we engage with the same five people and no one else. It's never too late to break out of that pattern, but to do

GET LOUD!

Since childhood, we've been told to "keep it down." But there's something freeing in letting yourself "break the sound barriers" that you've imposed on yourself. Here are a few ways to do it.

Sing gospel. Exercises the vocal cords, releases endorphins, lifts the spirit—what could be better? Just shed those inhibitions, walk into a nearby gospel church, say hello to everyone, take a seat in the back, and sing your heart out. Or if you insist on staying home, you can now purchase "gospel karaoke" music (honest).

Try "primal scream therapy." John Lennon and Yoko Ono helped popularize this years ago, and there are still therapists who use it as a technique. But who needs a doctor?

1. Shut yourself down in the basement.
2. Take a deep breath.
3. Scream.

Now repeat steps 2 and 3.

Yell down into a canyon. I promise, if you have not done this, you have no idea how much fun it is.

Get a megaphone. In the classic Jason Robards film *A Thousand Clowns*, the lead character keeps a bullhorn handy in his apartment so he can lean out the window at dawn and announce, "Okay, everybody report downstairs for volleyball!" His neighbors did not think it was funny, but he did, and that's what matters.

Play the drums. You were always told to stop banging on them when you were a kid, but there's no stopping you now. And if a full set of drums is too much, a modest set of bongos will do the trick.

so you have to shed your inhibitions and regularly put yourself out there in the mix, the way you probably did in younger, more social days.

BREAKING YOUR OWN RULES

I think a lot of shedding your inhibitions is about defying your own self-made stereotype and breaking the rules you've imposed on yourself. "I'm a pretty quiet person," you'll hear someone say about herself. That's a restriction that person has come to accept, and it gets reinforced every time that sentence is spoken. But here's the rule that person *should* be following: Even if you've been quiet for the past 20 years, it doesn't mean you must be quiet for the next 20. There are lots of little ways you can begin to make a racket. And every little noisy act of defiance will break down that stereotype some more.

If making noise seems out of character for you, well . . . *that's the whole idea.* There's no reason your character, and by extension your life, must be predictable and one-dimensional. A person can be both quiet *and* loud. A very responsible mother of two can also ride a motorcycle. In breaking out of your own mold every now and then, you make yourself harder to categorize, tougher to pigeonhole—and therefore more interesting. Not that it matters what others think anyway: If you're breaking the rules, you should be doing it for yourself, not for effect.

WHAT DO YOU HAVE TO SAY?

Once you've begun to loosen your inhibitions and lessen your fears of embarrassment, you may be ready to progress beyond bongo-thumping and the wearing of red hats and move toward making a personal statement that is bigger, more individualized, and more creative. But what should you say, and how should you say it? Let's start with the first part of that, the message. I think all of us have something to say, an issue that is important to us. In my own case, I have a burning desire to talk to people about living more fully and making a list of great experiences. This book is evidence of that, but the same message tends to come out in my television work, and I'm sure if I took up painting, the message would find its way into that form, too. It's a message that I feel compelled to share. Often, our messages come out of our own life experiences: what we've learned and what we wish to impart. The artist Anthony Papa (whose List for Life is featured in chapter 11) spent years in prison, where he learned to paint. He's been a free man for a long time, but his art

MAKING A GOOD IMPRESSION

Let's say you want to express yourself by creating art, but there's one small problem: You can't draw so much as a decent stick figure. No problem, says the artist and author Margaret Peot, whose book, *Make Your Mark: Explore Your Creativity and Discover Your Inner Artist*, suggests dozens of ways you can put an artful image onto a canvas or paper without any technical artistic or drawing skills. "I was finding that a lot of people want the experience of being a creator of art, but they don't have the time or desire to start learning basics like drawing the human form," she says. Peot's solution is to throw away that drawing pencil and grab the . . . *lemon juice?*

Indeed, one of the more unusual suggestions in the book is to spray lemon juice over a composition of dried flowers spread on a blank page.

continues to be driven by a message that speaks on behalf of prisoners everywhere.

Your message doesn't have to be as issue-driven or even as specific as that. Maybe it's just a feeling you have about sunsets, or perhaps it's something you can't even put into words. But chances are it does exist, inside you, and it's itching to come out in some form. Which brings us to the next question: What form? You may already know the answer to that question from past experience. Maybe all you need to do is dust off the old canvases and brushes, or tune up the old guitar. But if you don't know, finding your medium (or media—no one says it has to be just one) is a fun journey in itself.

As you search, keep an open mind about the possibilities. In the right hands, almost any material can be used to create art, and just about any-

Remove the flowers, heat the paper in the oven for a few minutes and, voilà, the lemon juice becomes visible to create what Peot describes as "a haunting image." Peot's book also shows you how to create art using the Japanese technique of Gyotaku—which involves making a print from a fish. You buy a fish from the market (with scales still on), use a foam roller to ink up the surface of the fish, place rice paper on top of it, apply light pressure, and you end up with an image of a fish that's both realistic and textured. Peot also shows how to create images using various types of stencils, ink blots, and rubbings (made by placing tracing paper against an object and rubbing with a black wax crayon). Once you've created these various images using natural objects, you now have something more than a blank canvas to work with; you can proceed to add your own personalized artistic touches by filling in those shapes, using colored pencils or inks, to create a finished work of art.

thing can be a canvas. In my own travels, I have encountered a number of unusual forms of self-expression, including:

- The "Car Beaters Club," whose members cover their cars with personal art

- A man who continues to work on the world's largest ball of barbed wire

TURNING ART INTO A LIVING EVENT

I like the idea of expressing yourself in a bold, larger-than-life manner, and I can't think of a better example of that than the "aerial art" of John Quigley. I came to know John recently when he approached N.O.W. TV and told us that his dream was to create an artistic image that would call attention to the plight of homeless veterans. That message certainly appealed to me, but what was really intriguing was the medium: a type of art known as "human pointillism." John explained it to me, but I didn't really grasp the scope and complexity of what he was trying to do until it was time for him to do it.

Like every N.O.W. dreamer, John was given 72 hours and a $3,000 budget to work with as he pursued his ultimate artistic creation. The first 2 days were spent gathering the raw material of his art. For human pointillism art, that raw material consists of . . . people. For this project, John needed hundreds of them, and to make the point he wanted to make, they all had to be homeless veterans. This required a massive outreach project, seeking out veterans in local shelters and busing some of them in from afar. John arranged for all of them to arrive, on day three, at the destination point—an open field in the Los Angeles area, where John had already begun to "lay the groundwork"

- A designer of "fighting mechanical art"

- A beer lover who built his house from beer cans

- An "aerial artist" who arranges people in a field to form an elaborate human mosaic that is photographed from above

Whatever form of self-expression you choose, there is only one rule I would urge you to abide by: You must go public. The masterpiece that

(continued on page 174)

for his artwork by inserting little markers in the grass. As the veterans assembled and stood drinking coffee in that field, John spoke to them about what he was trying to do and the message he was attempting to get across. Then he got down to the business of creating living art.

He asked each person to lie down in a designated spot on the ground. He then began arranging their arms and legs, just so. I was close by, observing with the N.O.W. TV cameras rolling, but I was unable to discern any pattern in what he was doing. Only John could see what was unfolding and taking shape, and the rest of us had to take it on faith that he really did know what he was doing. Eventually, John seemed satisfied with this massive arrangement of human figures splayed on the ground. It was at this point that a helicopter flew overhead, with a photographer on board taking pictures.

The veterans themselves didn't really grasp what they had been part of until they saw those photographs—which showed a field full of people positioned to form a perfect re-creation of that classic image of soldiers raising the flag on Iwo Jima. Everyone on hand, and especially the veterans, was deeply moved by the sight of this image. But John's hope was that the impact of his creation would extend much further in days ahead, as copies of the photographs were sent to government officials and media outlets—a bold, dramatic reminder to the powers that be that our veterans must not be forgotten or overlooked.

SHED YOUR INHIBITIONS/ EXPRESS YOURSELF: POSSIBILITIES

Because this chapter combines two themes, some of these possibilities deal more with "inhibition," some fall more on the "express yourself" side, and some are a combination of both.

Get naked. It could be the easiest, most powerful way to shed your inhibitions. Middle-aged British women are posing nude in calendars, crazy fans are running around nude in Nike ads, and the American Association for Nude Recreation reports that membership is on the rise (no jokes, please). You might consider posing as an artist's model (and maybe pick up a buck while shedding those inhibitions). Or you could pack light and set sail on a "nude cruise." Check www.nudetravelguide.com for listings on nude boats, beaches, and B&Bs (yes, that means nude bed-and-breakfasts).

Learn to love, and love to learn. This is risqué territory, but sex is an area where inhibitions loom large and some shedding may be in order. So much of what we learn about sex is shrouded in secrecy and guilt. The challenge is to get yourself to approach the subject with a more open and curious mind-set, and with the understanding that there's nothing "dirty" about learning to better express physical love to your partner in life. It's never too late to learn to do this in new ways, or "old ways," for that matter. The ancient Eastern practice of Tantra, which deals with tapping into sexual energy and expressing it freely, can be learned on DVD or in classes at local Tantric centers (www.tantra.com).

Perform live! No, we're not talking about sex anymore. We're talking about going "busking" as a street performer, going to a "spoken word" poetry club, or taking the stage on open-mike night at your local comedy club. And if you're too timid for all that, last but not least there's always . . . karaoke!

Be bad. Be very bad. The actress and free spirit Katharine Hepburn once said, *"If you obey all the rules, you miss all the fun."* The irresistible urge to break the rules and get away with it resides in a dark little place within all of us. It's an opportunity to defy not only our own inhibitions but society's as well. Of course, this book would never recommend that anyone actually trespass, but we have heard about an interesting diversion known as "pool hopping." You sneak into a yard, dive into the pool, and swim the length. Then you move on to the next yard and pool, until you've swum the neighborhood.

Stay up all night just because you feel like it. This was mentioned in the "childhood" chapter, too, but it bears repeating because it's so much fun. And as long as you're up . . . snack on junk food all night, too. But don't do this often, or you won't be in shape to do anything else on your List for Life.

Get your letter to the editor published. This is a way to get your message into the mainstream media. Instead of thinking about it, and verbalizing it across the breakfast table to your spouse, *actually write the letter.* The New York Times recently published an Editors' Note from Thomas Feyer, its letters editor, that gave readers suggestions to increase their chances of getting published. Feyer recommended that letter writers keep it short (150 words or less); pick an especially timely topic; and "write quickly, concisely, and engagingly."

Create crop art. I did this once and would love to do it again. I want to travel to the heart of rural America, perhaps to a big field in Nebraska. With the permission of the landowner, I will begin to cut a swath in that field, a line running 100 feet long, then another line slanting down, and then one going straight back up—to form an "N." Then I would carve the giant "O" and finish with the giant "W."

you create and then hide in the drawer does not qualify as a N.O.W. experience. Creating it is only part of the experience; the other part comes when it is brought out into the world and shared with anyone who will look. Self-expression requires an audience. Otherwise, you're just talking to yourself. Whether that audience is big or small, whether it includes harsh critics or even harsher mothers, you'll survive the exposure. In fact, you just might thrive on it.

9

BREAK NEW GROUND

S WE ARRIVE AT NUMBER 7 on your List for Life, it's a good time to take stock of what is on that list and, in particular, what's missing from it. We're getting down to the final two slots, so we need to make these last two themes count.

If you think about the six themes covered so far—facing your fear, losing yourself in another world, testing your limits, taking a leap of faith, rediscovering your childhood, and expressing yourself—there are certain elements they have in common. All, in a sense, are about reaching deep inside yourself and trying to locate something in there—buried fear, a neglected spirit of adventure, untapped resolve and resourcefulness, inner faith in yourself, childlike enthusiasm, and, finally, personal creativity. These are great qualities, and to the extent that you can come up with experiences that tap into these qualities, you stand to enrich your life immeasurably.

However . . .

There's something else these six themes have in common. They are, to borrow a phrase popular in Hollywood, *all about you, baby:* your needs and desires, your possibilities, and, ultimately, your satisfaction. There's nothing wrong with that; it *is* your life we're trying to expand via this list.

But at the same time, I believe a balanced List for Life should also look outward. It should consider how your experiences can affect and impact other people, not just in the short term but in the long run.

With that in mind, the last two themes we'll be looking at have a slightly broader agenda than the first six. They're still focused on helping you to pursue rich, memorable, once-in-a-lifetime experiences. But they recognize that a great experience can also involve helping, sharing, building, pioneering, inventing. Your great experience can touch others. It can leave a lasting impression on more than just your own memory. And all of this can serve to make it even more satisfying and enjoyable to you.

For the purposes of the list, this type of experience can be subdivided into two separate categories: sharing and building. Sharing dreams will be covered in the next chapter, Aim for the Heart. In this chapter, we'll focus on building, or breaking new ground. In the most literal sense, that could mean actually breaking ground to build a house that people can live in for years to come, or carving and crafting a chair that people will relax in for years to come. It can be a matter of making anything that can be useful to anyone. It can involve inventing something completely original—or tweaking something that already exists to make it more beneficial.

Another quite literal use of the term could involve planting or growing something in the earth, though if you want this to measure up as a N.O.W. experience, it should go beyond the mundane and personal. The lawn in your yard does not count, although it would if that yard served an entire housing project filled with people for whom a beautiful lawn would be a rare and special gift. There are many other possibilities having less to do with *making something* than with *making something happen:* for example, blazing a trail for others by starting or establishing a service or an activity that no one has done before, at least not in your community. All of this amounts to some form of breaking new ground.

Just as themes like "Test Your Limits" and "Get Lost" tap into deep, almost-primal needs, so, too, does "Break New Ground." In fact, it can satisfy several separate and distinct needs at once: the desire to "make" something by employing your own ingenuity, the longing to feel useful to others, and the wish to leave a mark or have a lasting effect. Unlike some of the more-fleeting experiences apt to be found on your list, this one has an element of permanence associated with it.

REJECTING THE "READY-MADE" LIFE

In a modern world where everything, it seems, is ready-made and pre-fabricated "for your convenience," our natural abilities to build and invent are often allowed to languish. Products and services have evolved to make everything easier—the idea being, if you just spend a few bucks, you won't have to lift a finger. But as human beings, we *want* to lift a finger sometimes. Something in us craves the challenge of constructing, of using our own hands and wits to solve problems, or to produce something that didn't exist before. Children tap into this from the time they start playing in the sandbox, and it continues throughout many inventive years of childhood. But for a lot of us, this spirit of ingenuity gets lost somewhere on the way to adulthood, or it becomes channeled entirely toward our careers. Eventually, we begin to leave the jobs of building and making to the professionals—the carpenters, the landscapers, the architects, and the engineers. In so doing, I think, we're cheating ourselves out of opportunities to be involved in something original, fundamental, challenging, and deeply satisfying.

If you think about previous generations in your family—probably your

So You Want to Make Wine for a Living?

Who among us has not had the urge to shuck the office life, roll up our sleeves, and go out and actually make something for a living? The possibilities are endless: You could make your own furniture. Your own jewelry. Your own hand-carved toys. Your own quilts. All worthwhile endeavors, but you and I both know you're not really going to quit your job and do this every day.

The solution? Become a weekend craftsperson. Set your sights on a particular seasonal craft show, festival, or street fair, and gear up for the event by working weekends making a lot of whatever you make, to build up a decent supply. Then rent yourself a booth at the fair and see what it feels like, for a day, to sell what you've made with your hands. If your entire inventory sells out immediately, then maybe you really should think about quitting your job.

Here's another way to test the waters: A new company called VocationVacations, based in Portland, Oregon (www.vocationvacations .com), allows you to try out certain kinds of jobs during your vacation. If you've always wanted to be a winemaker, for example, company founder Brian Kurth will arrange for you to spend a few days working with a real vintner to see what it's like. Or if you want to know what it's like to make chocolate or cheese, he'll put you to work with a chocolatier or cheesemaker. The package includes a follow-up session with a career coach to help you figure out if you really want to make the move or not. Kurth describes what the program offers as "baby steps into a possible new life."

parents, most definitely your grandparents—there's a good chance you may have recollections of people who often made things themselves and who also reused and adapted what was available to make it suit their needs. This was common behavior in times when resources were less plentiful and "doing for yourself" was a source of pride. The disposable economy had not yet evolved, and people were loath to throw anything away if there was any possibility of taking that old object or material and reinventing it, adapting it for a new use.

My grandfather was a classic example. He seemed to save everything, every little empty casing or spare hinge, in the belief that he could use it sometime, for something. It was amazing how often he was proved right about that. We have an expression Down Under—"That fellow can fix anything with a piece of number-eight wire"—and that was true of my grandfather, who could fix things even *without* number-eight wire. He often invented his own tools or modified existing ones to raise them up to his standards. "Don't like the handle on this," he'd say, and before you knew it, the object in question had been refashioned with a new handle. Some of his inventions were elaborate and ahead of their time. He was, to my knowledge, the first to build what's known as an "outrigger site" for a rifle, enabling a right-handed shooter to aim with his left eye (like a lot of my grandfather's creations, it was born out of simple necessity; he had a friend who was a competitive shooter and needed just such a device). My grandfather's resourcefulness no doubt came from his early life as a Kiwi frontiersman, but it never left him. Even after he was far removed from the frontier life and in a position to buy more things instead of making them, he chose the latter. He absolutely lived for those moments when he got to solve a problem using his mind, hands, and whatever scraps were available to him.

INVENT SOMETHING!

You know that idea of yours for the perfect widget—the one you've been telling everyone about for years? Stop talking about it, write it down on your list, and then begin the process of turning it into a reality.

It's not as hard as you might think: Every year, more than 100,000 ideas are granted patents by the U.S. government, and many of those ideas end up as useful, money-making products. "People tend to think everything's been done, but there are new inventions coming along every day and there's lots of room in the market for new ideas," says Randy C. Moyse, who runs the Inventors Headquarters Web site (www.inventorshq.com) and is the author of *The Inventor's Pocket Guide*. According to Moyse, "The simpler your idea the better. It should provide a very clear solution to a definite problem." Moyse's own best-selling invention is just a cardboard box—albeit one with adjustable slots specially designed to make postal deliverers' lives easier. He sells several thousand of those a month.

How do you turn your idea into an invention? Start by finding out if there's anything like it on the market. You can do your own patent search just by going to the Web site of the U.S. Patent and Trademark

I believe he passed a tiny shred of that quality on to me, though not nearly as much as I would have liked. Still, on those occasions when I've found myself behaving like my grandfather—by coming up with my own ways to adapt camera equipment so as to get difficult shots (I made my very own

Office (www.uspto.gov). Let's assume you can't find anything like your idea. Before you go to the trouble and expense of applying for your own patent, do some work on a rough prototype. "You have to turn your idea into something tangible," says Moyse, "even if it's just something pieced together with cardboard and duct tape." Once you've made a prototype, show it to friends and let them fool around with it. "And listen to their suggestions," says Moyse. People will help you figure out if it needs a button here or a wheel there.

When you've made your modifications, apply for your patent with the USPTO. If that governmental body determines that you have "invented or discovered any new and useful process, machine, manufacture, or composition of matter, or any new and useful improvement thereof," you will be granted (for a fee) a 20-year patent. Now all you have to do is figure out how to make a million bucks off your patented brilliance. Moyse says there are several ways to get your product out into the world: You can produce it yourself and then pay to offer it in catalogs; you can approach manufacturing companies directly (not surprisingly, smaller companies are likely to be more receptive to independent inventors); or you can work with a third-party marketing company that specializes in pitching new product designs to big companies.

"Kiwi-cam" by attaching a camera to the end of a pole for high shots, and also rigged a camera to flexible cables for "falling shots")—I've experienced flashes of that pride of invention my grandfather must have known all the time. And I can attest that it is a thrill I wouldn't trade for a bungee jump.

GOING FOR IMPACT

So what does this mean in terms of your own List for Life? That you can simply jerry-rig a contraption to use in your basement and then check off number 7 on the list? Well, I would suggest that as you try to come up with a Break New Ground experience, you should seek out more than just the thrill of invention. If you can find a way to build, invent, or initiate something that *also* serves a human need beyond

BREAKING GROUND DURING YOUR TIME OFF

Can you picture yourself wielding a shovel or a pickax during your vacation? If so, then a "volunteer vacation" or "service trip" may be the right experience for you. You get to travel to some of the most beautiful national parks and wilderness sites and then get to work, usually as part of a volunteer team supervised by a park ranger. Your job may involve clearing rivers and ponds or digging gullies to stabilize a mountain trail against erosion. It's hard work and you may have to pay to do it (airfare plus a few hundred bucks), but the rewards are many, volunteers say, including a feeling of "giving back" to nature, a sense of ownership in the areas you work on (volunteers often return to see how their work is holding up), and an opportunity for bonding with fellow "workers." The Sierra Club (www.sierraclub.org) offers volunteers a chance to work on mountain trails in Bryce Canyon National Park in Utah, an archaeological site restoration in New Mexico, and other outings. Similar programs are being offered by the Appalachian Mountain Club and The Nature Conservancy.

your own, you're on your way toward an experience that could potentially be not only satisfying but also meaningful and important. That may sound daunting, but there are countless possibilities out there. I know this because ideas of this nature have been coming in to the mailroom of *No Opportunity Wasted*, sent to us by imaginative dreamers who have suggested creative and fascinating ways to "build" a dream for themselves while also enriching the lives of others. For example:

If you're looking to go farther afield, you can try your hand at organic farming in Alaska's wilderness, or (this one I love) work on habitat reconstruction on the Galapagos Islands. Those are a couple of the exotic volunteer programs offered by the Global Volunteer Network (www.volunteer.org.nz), a New Zealand–based volunteer program that will put you to work for as long as you want in one of a handful of exotic locations around the world. There are many such international programs being offered. You can scope them out on the Web site www.idealist.org, the Web's largest volunteer portal. A stint with an international volunteer organization can serve as an ideal sabbatical: a chance to get away, immerse yourself in another culture, and perhaps build something in the process. But do your homework before signing up with any of these programs; some are more reputable than others, application costs vary, and the program may or may not pay for accommodations. Make sure the volunteer organization is verified with Idealist.org, and contact previous volunteers to see how they liked the experience.

• Veronica Reichhold, a single parent in St. Louis, wrote to tell us about her ongoing efforts to help build facilities for children in Jamaica. She's already been involved in creating a hatchery at one local shelter, and the next item on her List for Life is an ambitious plan to take an abandoned house on the island and completely rebuild it as a new kids' shelter.

• Dea Taylor, a Houston scientist who has studied the process of drilling water wells, wrote that her dream is to drill a well in a village in Zimbabwe, thereby providing people in the community with access to safe, clean drinking water.

• Duane Silverstein, whose interest is in marine ecology, wrote in with a dream to build a new coral reef on Bunaken Island in Indonesia, to help transform a barren dead reef into a living ecosystem.

• Garth Redwood, a martial artist and personal trainer in Los Angeles, wrote that he wanted to build and open a boxing ring in the poor neighborhood of Watts. Once the facility was built, he planned to use it to teach martial arts to local kids.

In several of these instances, people took a specific skill or knowledge they had—even something as arcane as knowledge of water wells—and figured out how to build an ambitious dream experience around it. Of course, even if you bring some expertise to the process, it can be a formidable challenge to build anything, particularly something that is lacking and much needed. (The very fact that the thing is lacking in the first place means there are probably reasons why no one has been able to build it previously. But then, no one ever said being a groundbreaker was easy.)

BUILD YOUR OWN CABIN

It's a dream harbored by many a city dweller: to go off into the woods, find a nice little vacant spot, and build a quaint cabin. That's what Mike Antoniak did when he left New York City almost 2 decades ago for the hills of Tennessee, where he proceeded to construct his new family home, log by log. Antoniak has since built three additional log cabin structures and has also written a book on the subject called *A Home from the Woods*. Building your own log cabin is hard work, Antoniak says, but he insists that anyone can do it and that the satisfaction that comes with a finished job is immense. "You get to see your own vision for a home come to life right in front of you," he says. "And it's a sense of accomplishment that stays with you and gets passed along: Someday my grandchildren will be able to say, 'Grandpa built this house.'"

Antoniak offers several tips for the would-be cabin builder. "Think it through before you start," he says, noting that you should be detailed in your diagrams and contingency plans. The second point is to "give yourself enough time," he says. "An artificial deadline may cause you to rush and make mistakes. Building a cabin takes longer than you might expect, especially if you have to learn to use the tools, as I did when I started out." Another tip: "Get help when you need it. It's great to feel you're doing it all yourself, but there are some parts of the job—such as electrical work—that may be beyond your skills." Finally, Antoniak says, "Enjoy the experience. Building a cabin is 'philosopher's work'—your mind is free to wander as you hew those logs."

THE FELLOWSHIP
OF THE RING

The *No Opportunity Wasted* TV series chose to follow and film one of the aforementioned dreamers, Garth Redwood, as he set out on his quest to build a boxing ring in Watts. His dream was rooted in personal experience, as so many of the best dreams are: Redwood had been a troubled youth from a poor background who often found himself getting into fights. When he discovered martial arts, it helped to change his life by giving him a discipline and focus he'd lacked. He felt that some of the underprivileged kids in the Watts neighborhood could benefit from similar training. To make this happen, he wanted to create a

CONSTRUCT A MUSICAL DREAM,
NOTE BY NOTE

Let's say you don't like to build houses or reconstruct natural habitats. Suppose what you're good at making is . . . music. If so, there's a way to custom-build a song for one specific person in need of a musical lift. Songs of Love (www.songsoflove.org) is a nonprofit organization dreamed up in 1996 by John Beltzer. A struggling songwriter at the time, his idea was to enlist other songwriters and musicians to create songs written specifically for individual children suffering from serious illnesses. Beltzer named the group in honor of his own musician brother, who, before his death 12 years earlier, had written a tune called "Songs of Love."

To date, more than 5,000 personalized songs have been written.

program and a training facility from the ground up, and he also wanted to have local kids involved in setting up and running the program. All of which were great ideas, but to accomplish them Redwood needed to deal with some hard realities. He had no place to set up the program, not much help at the outset, and (thanks to the ever-stringent requirements of our television series), not much time or seed money to get the job done.

With the clock ticking, he raced around the area in search of an available site. He went everywhere, it seemed. And everywhere he went, people wanted money from him. He was running into a wall of "no's" until someone introduced him to a Watts community leader named "Sweet Alice"—and she led Redwood into the valley of "yes." More pre-

Here's how it works: Beltzer receives information from hospitals about particular kids, including their names, names of family and friends, and some of their favorite things. Then he passes that information on to one of the many musicians who've signed up with the program, and they write a song with customized lyrics. The song is produced on a CD and then given to the child at the hospital. "We're learning that it's having a tremendous impact with these kids," Beltzer says. "Sometimes the hospitals even play the song while the child is receiving treatment, to keep his spirits up." You don't have to be a professional musician to participate in the program, but you should have access to a home music studio so you can produce a demo, which must demonstrate at least some aptitude for lyrics and music. After all, Beltzer says, "We don't want to send a kid a song that's so bad it's going to make him cry instead of smile."

cisely, she led him to an abandoned, cluttered yard with a tiny dilapidated garage space, which was offered free for the taking if anyone
could find a way to salvage it. Redwood looked at the sorry site and
shook his head, knowing he had his work cut out for him. With Alice's
help, he quickly rounded up more than 30 local volunteers, and they
began to dig, haul, sweep, and hammer. First the yard was cleared out;
then the ring went up, plank by plank, with a canopy built overhead for
shelter. Meanwhile, the small garage was restored and converted into
an equipment room. When the group was finished, what stood before
them was a thing of beauty. They paused and admired it, and someone
suggested they say a group prayer, which they did. Then Redwood
handed the key to the new equipment room to a surprised and very
proud teenager who'd taken the lead in organizing and rallying the volunteers on the project.

There are a couple of points worth noting here. Redwood discovered,
as one often does when trying to build something ambitious, that he
needed *a lot* of help. In fact, that is one of the great challenges of
breaking new ground in a big way: You have to rally others to the cause
and sell them on the vision of creating something that didn't exist before. You can look at this as a headache, or you can see it as an opportunity to create a spirit of teamwork and bonding that will only add to and
enrich your experience. Redwood definitely appreciated it as the latter.
By the end of the project, that "fellowship of the ring" was strong and
added to his overall positive feelings about the experience.

The other key point is that when Redwood and the rest of the group
laid down their hammers, folded their arms, and looked at their finished
project, they saw something that was beautiful to them *because of* the way
it was made. If there had been more money available, they could have

A Different Kind of "Groundbreaking" Experience

One way to break new ground is simply to come up with a completely original experience—something that (as far as you know) nobody's ever done before. It can be a little bit crazy; original ideas often are. Here's a one-of-a-kind experience that I took part in during a visit to Stromboli in Italy. I had come to see the active volcano located there. And I'd come for the fine Italian food, as well. So why not combine the two? It was decided that my companion, a local guide, and I would dine on a four-star gourmet meal atop the erupting volcano. To do this, we had to persuade a gourmet chef to climb up to the top of the volcano with us, and a waiter came, too. We packed everything we would need: food, dishes, cooking pans, cutlery, and olive oil.

When we reached our destination, overlooking the mouth of the volcano, the chef dug a little hole in the ground. This would serve as his oven (no need for a fire—the ground was so hot you could cook on it). When it grew dark, we lit candles all around, as we listened to the growing rumble of the volcano. I had changed out of my climbing clothes into a tuxedo, though I kept wearing my hard hat, just in case. We sat down at a table of flat rock covered in a fine linen cloth. The waiter brought an entrée of sautéed Scoffino fish and a delicate pasta, served with a goblet of fine Montepulciano wine. About midway through the meal, between forkfuls of pasta, the volcano erupted in all its blinding red glory. We sat back and watched, nodding appreciatively as we ate, just like dinner-theater guests. Then the volcano finished its performance, and we ordered dessert.

hired a professional team of contractors. And maybe those contractors would have brought in a tractor with a crane, which would have lowered a prefabricated ring onto that plot of land. That would have been the easy way to "construct" that ring. But if the ring did come into being that way, I don't think the group, and especially Redwood, would have had the same feeling as they stood before it.

IN PRAISE OF LIMITS

Again, this is why I happen to think those very limited budgets we provide to N.O.W. dreamers are a good thing. They force people to build instead of buying and to actually solve a problem instead of throwing money at it. One of my favorite quotes comes from the New Zealand–born scientist Ernest Rutherford, whose breakthrough work on splitting the atom was conducted in modest local research facilities. *"We didn't have money,"* Rutherford said, *"so we had to think."* That's what limited resources will do for you: push you to adapt and invent, to be more like my grandfather and his generation and less like a 21st-century "dependent."

The funny thing is that in today's world, people sometimes actually welcome having limits placed on them because they *want* to be challenged. Even though they may have more than enough money to buy an easy, ready-made solution, they're still hungry for a do-it-yourself experience, an opportunity to make or fix something using their wits and a bit of "number-eight wire." One of the people who wrote in to our show was a top dot-com entrepreneur, Jaymz Dilworth—a man swimming in Silicon Valley success and modernity. Yet his dream was to build a simple, handmade boat that he could then sail out to the Farallon Islands, off the coast of San Francisco.

We took him up on that dream, and over the 3-day filming period, Dilworth pulled together a team of friends who worked around the clock, putting together the vessel piece by piece with little more than lumber, glue, and fasteners. When it was finished, Dilworth set sail on this humble raft, like a modern-day Tom Sawyer. He got pretty far, though he didn't make it to his destination; a strong current pulled his boat astray and he eventually circled back home, drenched to the bone. But Dilworth was smiling all the way through the experience, having achieved immense satisfaction just by making that boat with his own hands. I asked him if he planned to take that raft out again, on another day. "Absolutely," he told me. Needless to say, Dilworth could easily afford to buy a boat capable of whisking him out to the Farallon Islands without a hitch. But he's chosen to cling to that simple raft. When he arrives at the island, he wants to know that he's been carried there by his own ingenuity and initiative.

That spirit of invention and ingenuity is inside all of us, though it may need some rekindling. If you can get that flame going just by building one small thing, you may find that one small thing leads to another that is larger; the urge to build will build upon itself. And it may just spill over into the way you live. When you become accustomed to being inventive, to adapting, you also become better at adapting to all kinds of difficult experiences in life. You become a natural problem-solver; you become *resourceful*. It's a good way to live, even in a world of plenitude. And it's a good example to set for children who will grow up in a world where—who knows?—resources may not always be as plentiful as they are today.

BREAK NEW GROUND:
POSSIBILITIES

I can't possibly tell you what it is you should build. I can offer a few general possibilities and suggestions to get you thinking. But you may want to follow the examples of some of the N.O.W. dreamers mentioned earlier, who began by considering their own unique skills and then looked for a situation where those skills could be applied to make something that was needed. In some shape or form, they already had a shovel. They just needed a place to start digging.

Build a tree house. In chapter 7, I recommended that you climb a tree. What I'm saying now is that maybe you should bring a hammer up there with you. A tree house is a great way to kick-start the builder within you. It can be as simple or elaborate as you want, and it's fun to work on because, hey, you're up in a tree. It's a great gift to your kids and their friends and maybe the whole neighborhood, though it can also be an occasional oasis for you—a great place to work on your List for Life. If you've never built one before, get a few tips from a carpenter or handyman, and check out the book *Treehouses* (Lyons Press). The author, John Harris, heads a tree-house construction firm, and he includes more than 20 examples of different types of houses in the book.

Build the ultimate sand castle. The sandbox is where a lot of us first "broke ground," with a little shovel and pail. You're too big for the box, so the beach will have to do. If you're serious, consider entering a sand castle competition to really push yourself. It takes a lot of imagination to win one of those. My wife, Louise, and I managed to pull it off one year by sand-sculpting a tennis match—court, net, players, the works. Check out www.sandcastlecentral.com for tips on contests and sand-carving tools, along with photos to inspire you.

Volunteer with Habitat for Humanity. Yet another dream on my long list is helping to build a house with this amazing organization. Yes, it's been around a couple of decades, and putting on the Habitat hard hat may not be as trendy as it once was, but the basic concept remains as sound as the houses themselves. You learn skills and get to try a "groundbreaking" experience, somebody in need gets a house, and everybody on the job gets to know one another. You can't beat it. You can sign up in your own city or travel afar, and Habitat for Humanity also has larger special projects worth looking into, such as the annual Jimmy Carter Work Project, in which the former president presides over an intensive 5-day project, building 100 or more houses in one shot. Women may be interested in the "Women Build" department, which can guide you to projects constructed entirely by women. Information is available at www.habitat.org.

Plant an urban garden. Urban gardeners find ways to make things grow in the most unlikely spots: rooftops, parking lots, abandoned fields. A popular technique for gardening on concrete is to use containers (such as plastic wading pools) filled with soil. Other gardeners use "found objects" (cinder blocks, old chests of drawers) as planters. An urban garden can be a source of community pride, but it can also be used for practical purposes, such as growing vegetables to donate to soup kitchens.

(continued)

(continued)

BREAK NEW GROUND:
POSSIBILITIES

Help renovate a school or community center. This may require some organization before you get down to the actual work (getting clearance from administrators, raising donations, gathering volunteers for the renovation), but that's all part of the groundbreaking process. A word to the fortunate: If your community's schools and recreation centers are already in tip-top shape, move down the road to the next neighborhood and you'll probably find plenty of work to be done.

10

AIM FOR
THE HEART

*SOMETIMES THE BEST WAY TO LIVE YOUR
DREAM IS TO HELP OTHERS LIVE THEIRS.*

OME MONTHS BACK, I walked into a classroom at a small Ohio college and asked one of the students, a woman I'd never met before, if she was interested in getting married. Not to me, mind you: I was speaking on behalf of her fiancé, Nick, who meanwhile stood fidgeting out in the hallway, alone except for a nearby janitor who was sweeping up. Inside the classroom, the young woman, Christina, was both stunned and thrilled. She'd wanted to marry Nick, but neither of them could afford a nice wedding, so they'd been putting it off. And now here I was, telling her that if she and Nick were ready to act immediately, the wedding of their dreams—an elegant affair worth thousands of dollars—would be entirely paid for and arranged by somebody else. I think she was ready to hug me until she learned that *I* wasn't the one arranging the wedding. "The person who is doing this for you," I told Christina, "is somebody you've never met. And this person wishes to remain anonymous."

While Christina tried to absorb all of this, I brought Nick into the

room. He proposed to Christina again, she accepted again, and they embraced. There were smiles and applause from the people watching,
which included myself, the class professor, the other students, and even
that janitor out in the hall, who was shyly poking his head in the door to
see what was happening. I felt happy for Christina and Nick, and so did
the others in the room. But I don't think any of us felt as good as that
janitor did.

The janitor, you see, wasn't really a janitor. He was a N.O.W. dreamer
by the name of Roger Cram. He'd written to us, months earlier, telling
us that his dream was to anonymously set up a beautiful wedding for a
young, deserving couple. This might seem an unusual thing for a person
to do, but not for Roger, who's been doing these kinds of anonymous
good deeds for years. In fact, Roger and some friends formed a group
they called the Secret Society of Serendipitous Service to Hal, or
SSSSH!, which is named after a friend of Roger's, Hal Reichle, who died
in the first Gulf War. "Hal liked to run around doing good deeds for
people without telling them," Roger explained to me when we met.
"He'd pay for someone's groceries, or shovel somebody's sidewalk when
they weren't looking." Roger decided to carry on the tradition, always
remaining anonymous and asking for only one thing from the recipients
of his good deeds: that they someday turn around and do a good deed
for somebody else.

The wedding idea was bigger than any other good deed Roger had
done previously, so he decided to approach our television show to see if
we wanted to film it and lend some support. When he came to us, he had
no idea how he'd arrange an elaborate wedding within the show's 72-
hour deadline; the only information he had at this point was the name
of the would-be bride. He'd searched around and talked to people lo-
cally, which is how he heard about 23-year-old Christina. Years earlier,

she had gone through difficult times, living on welfare at one point. But she turned her life around and was now going to college and working at a local homeless shelter to try to give something back to the community that had once supported her. As soon as Roger heard the inspiring story, he thought, "She's the one."

Once he received the go-ahead and the $3,000 budget from *No Opportunity Wasted*, Roger immediately swung into action, calling local shops and suppliers to get the wheels in motion on catering, flowers, photography, and the making of a wedding dress. To look into honeymoon possibilities, Roger went down to a local travel agency. "Do you have a price range for the trip?" the travel agent asked him.

"Well, actually," Roger said, "I want you to donate it."

He took the same direct approach with a number of other people, saying, in effect, "Everybody is pitching in because this is a good thing to do. Now how about you?" And the amazing thing is, many of those he approached quickly got into the spirit of the experience and in some cases went to great lengths to help. (The woman who agreed to make Christina's wedding dress worked through the night to get it done in time.) Roger, meanwhile, was a whirlwind during the 3-day period, his schedule broken down into precise 15-minute chunks so he could stay on top of everything. But he still found time for his own bit of fun and games. When Christina went to the jewelry shop to pick up her free wedding ring (donated by a friend of Roger's), Roger was once again hovering nearby in disguise—this time as a store security guard.

It all culminated in a beautiful wedding that Christina described as "a gift from God." She knew, of course, that the gift was from a mere earthly mortal, but in her mind, the mystery donor had become a kind of angel. "If people did this kind of thing for each other all the time," she said to me at one point, "just imagine how different the world would be."

As the ceremony ended, Christina and Nick learned that they would be whisked off to the Caribbean for a honeymoon. And there was even some spending money for them in the amount of $1,300—because Roger had been so successful in getting people to donate services that he spent only a little more than half of his N.O.W. budget. Needless to say, the bride and groom were ecstatic, the wedding guests were thrilled, and I was having a pretty good time myself. But no one was smiling more than the fellow off to the side snapping all the photographs. He'd arrived in a van that said "Uncle Charlie's Wedding Photography" on the side, but I could've sworn he looked just like a janitor I once saw.

How to "Ambush" Somebody

On the *No Opportunity Wasted* TV series, we've become experts at ambushing dreamers. Once we have selected an applicant and decided to film his quest to fulfill a dream, we don't give him any advance warning. We just show up somewhere, with cameras, so that we can ask point-blank: *"Are you ready to do your dream now?"* I have to say, I get quite a kick out of setting up these little dream-ambushes. It's a bit like organizing a surprise party—which, as we all know, can be as much fun for the organizer as it is for the guest of honor.

Let's say we're going to ambush John Smith. We usually start out by covertly contacting John's close confidantes—his spouse, friends, coworkers. We try to get them to maneuver John into position so that we can strike with the maximum element of surprise, plus decent camera angles. "Do you think you can lure John into that diner across the street at noon tomorrow?" I might say to a confidante. "And make sure he's sitting with his back to the door so he doesn't see the camera coming."

ROGER CRAM TRULY EMBODIES the spirit of this last "theme" chapter, in which we'll explore possibilities for the final—and, I believe, most important—slot on your List for Life. The phrase "Aim for the Heart" seems to fit this theme, which requires that you zero in on something that really matters to someone else and then take your best shot at turning that person's dream into a reality. This will no doubt be the most selfless of the *No Opportunity Wasted* experiences on your list. Even the last chapter's Break New Ground theme (about building something that may benefit others) is partly driven by *your* own need to build and create. But Aim For the Heart is entirely about the needs of others. It requires

Another part of the setup usually involves talking to John's boss at work. Because people have to start on the 72-hour quest right away, it's important for us to help provide a window of time in which they're cleared of other responsibility; this takes away their excuses. I've found that even the toughest bosses are agreeable to letting someone off for a couple of days to pursue his dreams (though a cynic might say, "Of course the boss wants to seem nice—it's on TV!").

If you're planning to ambush someone, your job is a little more complicated than ours, because you may have to figure out what the person's dream is (though it shouldn't be hard; most people talk about their dreams all the time). Once you've figured it out and you're ready to take action, you might consider following some of the steps we do. Try to clear the person's schedule, with the help of coworkers and family members. You can make some preliminary arrangements for the experience, but don't go too far (it's the other person's dream, after all). Then lay the dream out in front of the person—with witnesses around. And ask point-blank: "Are you ready to do this *now?*"

that you look outside yourself and into someone else's heart and mind as you work to figure out what N.O.W. experience you should try to share with that person.

Really, though, Aim for the Heart is about more than sharing one experience. I think it's about sharing the whole philosophy of *No Opportunity Wasted* and passing it around, or "paying it forward." Which is, in effect, what I am trying to do by way of this book and also the *No Opportunity Wasted* television series. I'm attempting to pass on and spread around a way of thinking about life, which basically says, "Your dreams are important and worth pursuing, now." Mind you, I don't claim original ownership of this way of thinking. In one form or another, people have thought this way for ages. But even if it's an idea that's been around forever, it needs to be restated from time to time. All of us need occasional messages reminding us to live more fully. I happen to be in a good position to be that kind of messenger, and I also love carrying the message. What I'm suggesting in this chapter is that you can do likewise, and that you'll probably find the act of carrying and sharing the message to be extremely satisfying.

But how do you go about delivering this message to other people? Is it enough to just offer a few words of encouragement, perhaps urging someone to write her own List for Life? Sometimes yes, sometimes no. There are times, I believe, when you can and should go further, giving an extra little . . . push. Or maybe a big push: As Roger showed, you can get pretty deeply involved in helping someone else to live out his dream—opening certain doors for him, removing obstacles that may have stopped him in the past. And the act of doing that for someone can, in itself, become your own rich, challenging N.O.W. experience, as it did for Roger. Does anyone doubt how much pleasure Roger must have gotten out of orchestrating that experience—testing his own capabilities, having childlike fun while wearing his disguises, seeing the smiling faces that resulted from his efforts?

It's interesting, too, that this kind of a selfless challenge can bring out the best in your own abilities and in the people around you. I have seen countless examples of people who seem almost transformed by the act of doing something for someone else—they become super-motivated, much more than if they were doing that deed for themselves. Suddenly, they find themselves ennobled by a selfless cause, and empowered as well. They begin to feel, as Roger did, that anything is possible. They have no qualms about shooting for the moon and asking everyone around to help out; after all, they'll tell everyone, *it's for a good cause*. When this kind of powerful positive force kicks into high gear, what often results is an amazing experience for everyone involved.

TAKING AIM AT SOMEONE ELSE'S DREAM

The first thing you must do in pursuing this kind of experience is set your sights on someone else's dream. Who might that person be? The most obvious answer would be someone very close to you: a spouse, a dear friend, a family member. When you aim for the heart of someone who's close to you, it can be easier to hit the mark, because you know this person well enough to understand what matters to her—what she really *should* be doing, and why she's somehow just not doing it. With that information, you have a head start in figuring out what needs to be done to turn that person's dream into a reality.

(continued on page 204)

REKINDLING THE ROMANTIC FLAME

We can't have a chapter called "Aim for the Heart" without addressing the subject of romance. If you've long wanted to create the ultimate romantic moment, the number 8 slot on your List for Life is the place to do it. Here are some possibilities.

Write a sonnet for your loved one. What's required: 14 lines, iambic pentameter, and a set rhyme scheme. The Web site www.poetrydoctor.org/sonnet.htm can provide tips and examples.

Make up a new anniversary to celebrate. The wedding anniversary is too obvious. How about celebrating the anniversary of your first kiss? (If neither of you knows the exact date, then just guesstimate.) Or the anniversary of the day you proposed? Or the first time you went out to dinner?

Relive special moments. Don't just celebrate them; bring them to life again. The first movie you saw together? See it again, and watch it the way you did back then: popcorn, hand-holding, the works. Go back to the restaurant where you had your first romantic dinner. Go back to the actual physical place where you first met, and meet there again.

Have dinner in an amazing place. Perhaps on top of a volcano (you'll recall from the previous chapter that I did have a meal above a volcano, but unfortunately Louise was not with me; doing that together is on our list). Or on an ice floe, a suggestion that came to us from a N.O.W. dreamer. Or in the middle of the rain forest—up a tree, perhaps. Dinner can be simple, but the wine should be complex.

Or have dinner at home. But first, transform your home. With a little effort, you can set up an elaborate dinner in the backyard with candles and exotic plants and violins playing softly on a boom box hidden in the bushes. (And when the dinner's over, sleep outside, under the stars.)

Renew your vows in a memorable way. Renewal-of-vows ceremonies are popular these days, with lots of people arranging formal events that resemble a "wedding sequel." But my thinking is, if you've already had a standard wedding and reception, why not try something different for the renewal? As I mentioned previously, my wife, Louise, and I renewed our vows underwater (with Banana George bearing the rings), and I'll always treasure the experience. Sometimes an overall great experience has a particular N.O.W. moment embedded in it. In this instance, we had just completed the underwater ceremony and were still down there, kissing through our scuba masks, when a surprise guest appeared. It was a wild dolphin, which came swimming, as if on cue, right up to Louise and me and then circled around us a couple of times before disappearing. It was as if he'd just stopped by to give his blessing.

A footnote: I think that too often, single people are excluded from celebrations of romance, which should not be the case. If it so happens that you're not part of a couple right now, it doesn't mean you should deny yourself the basic human pleasure of romantic, sentimental moments, or miss out on the kind of hedonism that lovers get to enjoy. So go ahead: Buy yourself flowers. Surround your bathtub with candles, pour yourself a glass of something Italian, and put something French on the stereo. On your way to the tub, grab a copy of something written by Nicholas Sparks. And while you're soaking in bubbles, luxuriate in the pure pleasure of pampering yourself. You deserve it.

Case in point: One of the N.O.W. applicants who wrote to us, Gabe Cohen, told us that his dream was to help fulfill the nearly forgotten dream of his wife, Imelda. Years earlier, Imelda had gone to the prestigious Juilliard School in New York City, and her professional music career as a singer and guitarist was just starting to pick up when she agreed to move with Gabe to Chicago so that they could live closer to his family. From that point on, Imelda's musical ambitions were largely left behind in New York City. Gabe felt guilty about that. He wanted to do something to help Imelda realize her own dream to be a star musical performer, if only for one night. "My wife is so talented," Gabe wrote, "it would just be a waste if her music never was heard."

Gabe's dream was to secure a night at one of the most esteemed concert halls in Chicago, where Imelda's name would be posted in lights on the marquee. As he envisioned it, she would take the stage and perform before a packed house. There would be a rousing ovation at the end, and maybe even an appearance by a record producer backstage, asking Imelda about her future plans. It was a fantasy, no doubt about it, but Gabe wanted to make it real.

With my camera in tow, I ambushed him in Chicago one evening and asked him if he was ready to pursue his dream. Almost immediately, he was on the phone calling entertainment venues around town. And by the following morning, he had secured one of the most well-regarded concert halls in Chicago, the Aragon Ballroom. Gabe talked the manager into giving him a break on the cost of booking the venue. When the manager heard what Gabe was trying to do, he said, "Other people have helped me with my dream, and I want to help you with yours." (There's a lesson here: Never be shy about telling someone you're pursuing a dream, especially if that person is in a position to help you.)

Once Gabe had secured the hall, he faced the challenge of filling its 4,200 seats. He and his friends blanketed the city with posters and flyers. He hung out of a car window and yelled through a bullhorn. He tried every street-level promotion tactic he could think of to get the word out about the show. He knew that he needed to get on the radio but was having trouble getting through on the phone to the station he'd targeted. "Why don't you just go down to the station and see what happens?" I suggested. He did. And as it happened, there was an opening in the schedule that day and the producers must've taken pity on the guy hanging around outside: Gabe ended up getting on the air for a few minutes and plugged Imelda's concert. Inspired by his success at the station, he went down to the offices of a record producer and planted himself at the front door, begging for a meeting. This time it didn't work; they shooed him away, proving that dreams do sometimes bump up against harsh reality.

Speaking of which, I do wish I could say that the house was packed that night for Imelda's performance. But, in fact, only a few hundred people showed up. Friends, family, and anyone who cared about Gabe and Imelda were there, but strangers who'd only seen the flyers or maybe heard a blip on the radio opted not to show, which was perhaps to be expected. Gabe was a little disappointed by the turnout, though Imelda seemed relieved—less pressure on her performance. For her, the dream was just getting on a stage, and Gabe had secured for her one of the best in town. I think the most special moment for the two of them happened just before the show, when they walked into the Aragon green-room and sat in the same chairs that the Rolling Stones once sat in before a show. Imelda realized then that she was stepping into the big time on this night. When the curtain went up and she was alone in the spotlight on that grand stage, she responded with a beautiful and flawless performance. Which was the second half of her dream—to prove that once she got on that stage, she could handle it.

Of course, Gabe knew all along that Imelda could do it. She just needed that little push onto the stage. Whether this will restart Imelda's music career remains to be seen (Gabe did succeed in getting a demo tape of her music to the producer Clive Davis), but in any case, she came away with a N.O.W. experience—as did her husband.

PAYING TRIBUTE

"Our father was our best friend and biggest hero in the entire world," began the letter to *No Opportunity Wasted*, written by Sarah and Stephanie Wibracht, both in their mid-twenties. "We loved him, still love him, with a love so deep it cannot be explained with any words. With a love so deep that when he died, we couldn't feel anything but numb." The Wibracht sisters had lost their dad, Steven, in a scuba-diving accident just months earlier. They wrote to *No Opportunity Wasted* because they were seeking a bold, memorable way to honor this adventurous man who had inspired others around him and who always lived his own life to the fullest.

Just before his death, the sisters had been planning an adventure trip with their father, as they'd done so many times in the past. In fact, the house was full of new sleeping bags and camping gear their father had bought, just for that trip. So here is what the sisters decided: They were going to go ahead and take that last adventure trip with their father. Their mother—who used to always stay safely behind when father and daughters did their climbing, jumping, and diving—would

CONNECTING WITH
STRANGERS

Though an experience involving your spouse or partner or sister or best friend might seem to be a logical choice, there is also something to be said for sharing a dream with a person you don't know very well, or maybe don't know at all. Giving to strangers is the purest form of

be joining them on this particular journey. (And I was honored that they allowed the N.O.W. TV cameras to come along, too.) Together, the sisters and their mother proceeded to do all the kinds of things Steven Wibracht would have loved—including a skydive from a plane (which was a first for Mom) and a night camping together on a deserted Hawaiian beach, using a borrowed tent. When the adventures were done, the three of them spread Steven's ashes on a beautiful windswept beach as the sun set on the Nepali coast. They were joined by a Hawaiian priestess, who helped them bid a unique farewell to a unique man.

I won't soon forget the Wibracht sisters' tribute to their father, because it was a moving reminder to me that it is possible to share a dream with people even after they are gone. That's worth bearing in mind as you fill in this last slot on your list. If there's someone you've lost who meant the world to you, think about whether there might be some bold, unique, and appropriate way to honor this person through an experience. Don't think of it as an elaborate farewell but more as a celebration of someone special—and a way to keep his or her flame burning on in your life.

giving—there is no sense of obligation, no expectation of getting something back. Roger Cram and his friends at the Secret Society of Serendipitous Service to Hal have come to appreciate the pleasure of anonymous giving, and the group offers tips on how to make a stranger's day. Other people are also finding interesting ways to connect with strangers by sharing some special gift or token.

The person you choose to share a dream with is, of course, up to you,

SSSSH! DON'T TELL ANYONE YOU'RE DOING THIS!

Here are some ideas for anonymous good deeds, courtesy of the Secret Society of Serendipitous Service to Hal (http://home.hiram.edu/hal). The group recommends that when possible, you should leave behind a card explaining that an anonymous good deed has been done in the service of the late Hal Reichle.

- While in a restaurant, pay for the meals at another table. Ask the waitress to give you that table's check, quietly, and deliver to that table a "Hal" card.
- Cut someone's grass. (This was one of Hal Reichle's favorites.)
- Wash someone's car. (SSSSH! once did this in a parking lot and the car owner subsequently wandered around unable to recognize his own car.)
- Scrape, prime, and paint someone's garage or toolshed.
- Pay the food order for the car behind you in a drive-through fast-food restaurant.

but I do have some opinions about *how* best to share a dream. This is something we've thought a lot about at the *No Opportunity Wasted* TV series, because bringing other people's dreams to life is the point of the show. And the approach we've developed is as follows: *Don't* try to live people's dreams for them. *Don't* hold them by the hand or make it too easy. *Don't* hand the experience to them gift-wrapped. The idea is simply to get a person started on doing it for himself. You may make a few pre-

- Pay for the toll of the car behind you on a toll road.
- Pay for the movie of the third person behind you in line at the theater. It needs to be the third person so you can get away in time.
- Give a $50 tip to a bagger in a grocery store, explaining that she helped Hal Reichle several days ago and Hal forgot to tip her.
- Do the same for a waiter, saying he'd waited on Hal previously and Hal forgot to tip.
- Make arrangements to pay someone's gas, water, telephone, or electric bill. Call the utility company and offer this for a total stranger.
- At the dry cleaners, pay for someone's cleaning. Ask the clerk to give the person a "Hal" card when she arrives to pick up her clothes.
- Go to a nursing home and take a perfect stranger out for lunch, or bring an anonymous bouquet of flowers accompanied by a "Hal" card.
- Decorate for Christmas a small, isolated, miserable-looking tree or shrub near an area frequented by lots of people.

RETURNING SOMETHING THAT WAS ONCE CLOSE TO THE HEART

You never know where or when you may encounter an opportunity to connect with people in a deep and meaningful way. Martha Roskam stumbled upon one such opportunity at a small souvenir stand in Saigon a few years back. The Illinois woman had accompanied her husband to Vietnam on a business trip and was browsing for trinkets to bring home to her grandkids. She noticed a basket with metal tags, and upon closer inspection realized they were American soldiers' dog tags. "I picked some of them up and looked at them, and I felt a profound sadness," she says. "I knew there was a story behind each one of those tags. And it didn't seem right that they should be sold on the street as souvenirs."

Martha initially left the tags with the vendor and moved on, but kept thinking about them, and later discussed them with her husband. "You should go back and get them," he said, and she did, buying up the whole batch of 37 tags for $20. The plan was to bring them back to the United States and try to return them to the soldiers or their families. "I thought it would just be a matter of making a few phone calls," she says.

What she learned is that there is no easy way to return soldiers' dog tags, other than by doing the hard work of locating and tracking down

liminary arrangements on his behalf, free him from some obligations if that helps, and basically open a door for him. Then you ask him—challenge him, really—to walk through that door. "You know you've each individual soldier or family, 30 years later. Martha relied on her son Peter, an Illinois state senator, to help her sort through bureaucratic records and find addresses to match up with the identification on the tags. She also got help from a private detective, who donated his time when he learned what she was trying to do.

It turned out that four of the tags belonged to soldiers who'd died in the war. Martha first sent letters to these families, and three of those four returned her message and said they were interested in getting the tags back. But Martha and her husband didn't want to just send the tags by mail, so they decided to visit each of the families and personally return the tags. "It was very emotional meeting those families and bringing them something that belonged to those boys who were lost," she says.

Those family members were touched by the Roskams' efforts: "I can't believe they are going through all of this for people they don't even know," said the aunt of one of the slain soldiers.

As of today, more than 2 years later, the Roskams have returned nine of the tags to families or, in some cases, to the living soldiers themselves. "We've personally met all nine of those families," Martha says, "and we keep the letters we've exchanged with them. It means a lot to us." As for the remaining tags, she says, "We'll keep trying to return them to where they belong."

always wanted to do this," you might find yourself saying. "Well, here is your chance: Are you ready to give it a try?"

I think it is about the best gift you can give someone—an opportunity.

AIM FOR THE HEART: POSSIBILITIES

There are so many possible ways to share dreams with people that it's hard to know where to begin. Let's start with things that are easy to share and then work up to the harder stuff.

First, how about a hug? What could be easier? Recently, a Wall Street financial analyst decided that he would share a hug with any New Yorker in need of one, so he set up a giant hand-lettered sign announcing "Free Hugs" and began to embrace people every Sunday afternoon in Washington Square Park. Some people thought he was weird. Some suspected his motives. But hundreds of people took him up on the offer. I'm not suggesting that you set up a "Free Hugs" stand in your town (though come to think of it, why don't you?), but you could at least start with the people you know: family, friends, coworkers. It's a good exercise in getting used to sharing a little bit of yourself with people. And guys, no need to feel squeamish: Just use the "three-tap" back-patting hug, which is considered very manly.

Now, try sharing a book. I love the idea of taking something that means a lot to you personally and sharing it with a complete stranger. For example, a growing number of people have taken to leaving their favorite book on a park bench for someone else to discover and enjoy. And if you want to keep track of where that book goes, there is now a way to do that through the Web site www.bookcrossing.com. Here's how it works: Before you leave the book on a bench, register it with the site and write into the book an ID number and instructions to visit the Web site. With luck, people who find the book will post information on its whereabouts as they continue to pass it along. Then again, maybe you don't need to know all that—it can be more fun to just imagine where your book might be now.

Offer to join someone as they face a fear. Remember the story of Shane Platt facing the sharks in chapter 3? I don't think Shane could have done it without the help of his friend Ron, who accompanied him on the trip and even got into the shark-infested water with him. I know I said you shouldn't hold someone's hand throughout an experience, but you can, in fearful circumstances, back him up. For example, if he's scared to get up in front of an audience to do stand-up, you can offer to go up there with him—and be the Abbott to his Costello.

Stage a "this is your life" reunion for a friend. Do it right: Script it like a major extravaganza, and include a full band that is especially skilled at drumrolls and "ta-da's." Include "special mystery guests" (the long-lost college buddy, the third-grade teacher), who should first appear wearing funny masks.

Enroll your mother-in-law in cooking school. Your mother-in-law will thank you. Your spouse will thank you. Your stomach will thank you. If you really like your mother-in-law, send her to the best culinary institute in the state. If you don't like her, send her to the best in the world (that'll keep her in France for a while).

Knock your uncle for a loop. Okay, this applies specifically to my wife's uncle, Michael, but if you change a few details, it could apply to lots of uncles. Michael always talked about wanting to go up in one of those old Tiger Moth biplanes and fly loop-de-loops in the sky. I knew he wasn't ever going to do it without a push. So on his birthday we arranged to book a biplane with a pilot who knew how to fly loops. Then we drove Michael out to the airfield, without telling him what was going on. When we got there, he said, "You flying somewhere?"

And I said, "No . . . but you are."

A short time later, Michael was being turned upside down and inside out in that little plane. He came back to us slightly green in color,

(continued)

(continued)

Aim for the Heart

but also proud and thrilled. I took photographs of the whole experience. And now instead of telling people about how he'd like to fly loops in a plane, Michael just points to those photographs, displayed prominently in his house.

Donate yourself. Now we're moving up the ladder to more-challenging ways to share. Giving money is very noble, but giving yourself is very N.O.W.—you get to help, and you gain an experience as part of the deal. Here are two possibilities: Mentoring is a way to provide support and friendship to a young person, but it's also a chance for you to share some specific skill or knowledge that you have. Check in with www.mentoring.org for more details. Reading stories to seniors is another great way to share yourself; you can do this through local retirement communities or assisted-living centers. I once knew someone who had developed a whole routine for the seniors he visited, complete with stories, photos, and little quizzes he gave the audience. I believe he was a frustrated game-show host, and this provided a way for him to live out that experience.

Help something stay alive. What's a more important gift to share than life itself? You can build amazing experiences around the mission of helping wildlife to survive. How would you like to guard endangered turtle eggs from poachers in Costa Rica? (For more information, visit Reef and Rainforest Tours at www.reefandrainforest.co.uk.) Or to become part of the Monarch Butterfly Sanctuary Foundation (www.mbsf.org), whose efforts in Mexico help to protect the winter home of monarch butterflies? And then there's this idea, submitted by one of our N.O.W. dreamers: Stage a fancy dog show with dogs rescued from death row. Donations raised at the show would be used to house and feed the dogs until they are adopted.

11

THE DREAMERS
ALL AROUND US

THERE COMES A CERTAIN point in every race, in every climb, in every leap. It is beyond the point of no return: You're well past the middle and on your way into the stretch run (or the final ascent to the top, or the big landing at the bottom). It is at this point—if you happen to be accompanied by others taking the same run, climb, or leap—that you might turn your head, just for a second, to see how those others are doing. It's a chance to measure yourself, to be inspired by peers, and to know that you're not alone as you push onward.

That's the point we're at now, as we head into chapter 11 and the home stretch on the run to a N.O.W. life. At this point, you've worked your way through the eight great themes, designed to help you construct your own eight-point List for Life. As you finished each of those theme chapters, you presumably wrote a specific, personalized dream or goal on your own list. Which would mean that as of now, you have a completed, well thought out List for Life in front of you, and you are satisfied that these are the ideal dreams to pursue in your life ahead.

Maybe.

Then again, maybe not. At this point in the journey, there may still be some uncertainties; you may have one or two stubborn blank spaces on that list in front of you. Or perhaps you've written in some things hesitantly in light pencil, to serve as placeholders until you can think of something better. If this is the case, don't be discouraged: You've still got time to kick it up a notch. This chapter can be thought of as that point at which you look around, take stock of how far you've come, and gather yourself for one last push to complete your list—to tinker with it, fill in the gaps, bolster the weak spots. (In truth, you'll have the rest of your life to work on and improve the list, because this is a document that should change and grow as you do throughout your life. But let's just say you've got only one more chapter to go, in order to complete the *first full version* of that list.)

You may still need a few more ideas—and though you've been pelted with quite enough of mine already—this seems to be a good time to share examples of the dreams other people are pursuing in their own lives and on their own lists. It's a chance to pause on your way to the finish line and look up and around, to see how others are doing.

As I've mentioned previously, the *No Opportunity Wasted* TV series has received scores of fascinating dreams written in from people across America, and we'll peek at a handful of those dreams later in the chapter. But for this book, my coauthor, Warren, and I wanted to see what we'd get back if we reached out and asked people in various occupations and life circumstances to compile Lists for Life. It should be noted that these people weren't given 10 chapters' worth of exhortation and examples. We pretty much ambushed them and asked them to compile their dreams on the spot. Some seemed to have their lists already preformed in their heads, ready to spill out and fill eight slots; others had to work at it a bit.

A NUN ON THE RUN

Among those we approached was the remarkable Sister Madonna Buder of Spokane, Washington (profiled in chapter 5), the 74-year-old nun who still competes in triathlons. She holds a number of world records in her sport, but Sister Madonna is interested in more than athletics. Here is her List for Life.

Test your limits. "I think I'm going to try to set the world record for my age group (70–74) in the Hawaiian Ironman. This record has eluded me for 3 years for various reasons—last year it was stomach trouble. But I'm turning 74 now, so this will be my last chance to do it. I'm already the oldest woman to just finish the race, but that doesn't satisfy me. I want that record.

Face your fear. "I had to face it in my first Ironman competition. When it came to the swimming part, I was afraid of going into the water en masse, with all those bodies flailing around. It just scared me for some reason. But the apprehension was much greater than the reality. When I went into the water, it wasn't nearly as bad as I thought it would be. It just proves that a lot of times our fears are based on something that exists only in our minds.

Get lost. "I do this whenever I travel to triathlons held in different countries around the world. I always travel alone, and if I can stay with the locals rather than in a hotel, I do it. I want to take on the color of the place. Also I get out there and reconnoiter, as I call it. I try to find little unusual places that people haven't noticed.

Express yourself. "I would like to publish a series of children's books, called 'Adventure Alphabet Stories.'

Rediscover your childhood. "I like to invent games. That's what kids do so well—they invent, they use their imagination. I just made a game recently. I was taking care of some at-risk girls as a Sister of the Good Shepherd, and I got them all to play "snow ball." It's like baseball and you use a bat, except the pitcher throws snowballs.

Break new ground. "For the past couple of years I've helped with Habitat for Humanity. I love to hammer nails, paint, all of it. And I brought a teenager with me on the project so he could learn how to do that stuff.

Aim for the heart. "When I get too old to do triathlons myself, I'd like to work with the Special Olympics as a coach.

Take a leap of faith. "I do that all the time. If I didn't have faith, I wouldn't be doing any of these things."

A CHIROPRACTOR
REACHING NEW HEIGHTS

Another person you may recall from earlier in the book is Mitu Banerjee, whom you met in chapter 3. I helped her rappel down the side of a bridge to face her fear of heights. Having seen her accomplish that, I wondered what other challenges might be ahead for this 31-year-old chiropractor from Indianapolis. Here is her List for Life.

Face your fear. "Before I rappelled off the New River Gorge Bridge in West Virginia, I always had a fear of heights and I just couldn't understand why people would want to jump out of an airplane or parasail for fun. Well, I can tell you that I loved the "high" I felt after conquering that fear. I soon decided to go on a small four-seater airplane ride. I've never liked the idea of a small rickety plane—but if I could dangle myself over 200 feet, how could I not do something like this? I loved it. My next height-conquering adventure will be parasailing. Can't wait!

Get lost. "I have family and friends in India, and I have immersed myself into that culture so deeply on my vacations that I end up lost in another world. It makes you really appreciate what you have in your life in America; many people there don't have running water, and it's not uncommon to see a family of three or four on one scooter! I love to get myself lost in another culture because I believe that is how we grow.

Leap of faith. "After years of putting it off, I've started writing a kids' picture book. I'm unsure of the outcome—that is why it's a big leap of faith for me.

Rediscover your childhood. "Growing up, we moved quite a bit, but my most vivid memories of childhood are from when we lived in Denver. I loved to roller-skate there. My ideal experience would be to roller-skate in the same neighborhood I grew up in. I haven't visited Denver since we moved, but I hear that the neighborhood has changed completely. I would like to knock on the door of our old house and see it once again and re-live the memories of times with friends and family.

Shed inhibitions/express yourself. "I would love to hold classes or seminars to teach the public about chiropractic. This would not only help me improve my ability to speak in front of a large audience, it would give me a chance to educate people about what I love to do, and also help them to live a healthier lifestyle.

Break new ground. "My sisters and I once started a small dog-walking business, putting up signs around the neighborhood. It was no booming business, but we had a small clientele and I was very proud of that. These days, my goal is to open a chiropractic office that is so unique that it would draw people to come and see what we're doing. There are many ideas out there that have not made it into the market, and I would love to take some of those ideas and break new ground."

A RETURNING
SOLDIER'S DREAMS

I thought it would be interesting to ask a soldier just back from Iraq to share his List for Life. After a 1-year stint serving in Iraq, Jeff Risley, 36, is now back in his job in the post office in Rochester, New York. He shared dreams of today and, mostly, dreams of a year ago.

Here is Jeff's list.

Test your limits. "Going to Iraq for Operation Enduring Freedom might not have been my ideal location in my dreams, but I'd have to say I faced challenges that stretched my limits to the max.

Shed your inhibitions. "I've always wanted to be in a band—the lead singer. Although my grandmother said I was lousy during karaoke at a wedding. With all the background noise, I'm sure I would sound better than half the heavy metal garage bands playing at the average club.

Express yourself. "If I could, I would tell the soldiers still there that they are doing an outstanding job in Iraq and that the people back here support you a hundred percent. The day I returned home, my family and I stopped for a bite to eat. When we went to pay for the food, the manager told me one of his customers already paid and left. I thought that was a great thing to do.

Revisiting old dreams. "Instead of listing things I'd like to do someday, I thought it would be more interesting to go back to May 2003 when we first arrived just south of Baghdad, and make a list of what my dreams were at that particular time. My dreams consisted of the "little" things that we take for granted in normal everyday life, such as:

> • Ice: At 120 degrees and sometimes hotter, this was the number
> one object that I wanted. We had bottled water (which I know is

something our grandfathers didn't have during D-Day), but just 1 hour after the sun came up, water turned the same temperature as a cup of coffee. We would put the bottled water into a sock and tie them to our Humvee mirrors while we were driving, to keep the water cool. Our first experience with ice cost us $20 for a small block. We jammed it into a small cooler, and the rest we put onto our bodies.

• Food: Every night while waiting to go on duty, we'd come up with our "fantasy dinner." Keep in mind that at this time, our average weight loss was 30+ pounds. Each soldier in my unit would take turns choosing the menu: "prime rib, mashed potatoes, etc.," but the meal was always topped off with a Labatt Blue beer (in a frosted mug!). I believe that after we shared our fantasy dinners, morale would actually improve, although food never appeared.

• Freedom: Being locked down in a camp with no chance of escape from the reality of combat, I missed my freedom. Though we were sent to Iraq to protect America's way of life and freedom for every citizen, the American soldier has to be willing to give up theirs. But what I wouldn't give to be able to jump into my car and leave for the weekend to get away. Come back on Monday morning all fresh and ready to fight.

• Normal life: I'd have to say the majority of thoughts over in Iraq consisted of just wanting "my life" back. Just to be back with my wife and children, enjoying each other to the fullest. Because life is short, which is something we've all heard—but after living in Iraq and experiencing combat, that isn't just a cliché. It is the truth. So take advantage of every opportunity, and live life to the fullest!"

A SCHOOLTEACHER'S LIST

Speaking of heroes, I've always thought the unsung ones in our world are schoolteachers. They help all of us to prepare for the future—but what do they look forward to doing in their own lives? Kevin Walsh, 40, a public school teacher in the Detroit area, works with a large percentage of special-needs students and inspires them with his own passion for the English language and for film. Here is his List for Life.

Break new ground. "I'd like to create a high school that merges senior-citizen and day-care facilities with teenagers. I've found that teenagers act much more responsibly when given real responsibilities. Also, this system couldn't help but build more empathy between the teens and seniors—two groups that often clash and thus hurt voter support for public schools.

Get lost. "Working with poor children in Africa would be an excellent "island" on which to help others and learn how fortunate we are in America. While also helping to improve our current rotten foreign image.

Test your limits. "I would like to complete a novel with confidence, then have the determination to keep trying until I find a publisher.

Rediscover your childhood. "I've always regretted not taking piano lessons when I had the chance at age 8. But now I think I'd be able to make it through those lessons without dreaming about playing ball with my buddies instead.

Take a leap of faith. "I'd like to take a year off with my family to volunteer to work in a national park.

Shed your inhibitions. "To get over an innate fear of hurting someone's feelings, I would like to spend a week in a Middle Eastern marketplace where haggling over a price is part of the deal.

Aim for the heart. "My father died suddenly when he was 57 and had only really gotten to know one grandchild who was just 2 years old. I created a DVD of "Jim's Greatest Hits" that would allow his future grandchildren to press a button on the screen to relive one of his best moments we'd captured over the years on home video. After I'd assembled all the video, I took clips of those moments and put them together in a montage to his favorite song. All the clips worked perfectly to the music, and it still chokes me up today."

AN AD MAN AND A SURVIVOR

Some of the most interesting lists came from people who have gone through—or are still going through—a difficult life challenge. For example, Mike Hughes, 56, one of the most admired figures in the world of advertising (he runs the celebrated company The Martin Agency in Richmond, Virginia), has battled cancer and survived the loss of a stepson. Hughes noted that in his life, he has also enjoyed the thrills of scuba diving, bungee jumping, going on safari, and seeing exotic parts of the world. "I have a great marriage and family, a great job and great opportunities," Mike writes. "I am an incredibly lucky man. So where do I go from here? I've never lived my life off of a plan. But I do have things I think about. The first two items come from significant events in my life."

Here is Mike's list.

A deeper understanding. "Two-and-a-half years ago, after a long fight with AIDS, my stepson Preston died. While he was alive, I tried to get involved in AIDS causes but without much success. It was too hard. My wife and I gave some money, but I didn't really give of myself. Preston and I had a very good, very lively relationship—we clearly loved each other. But I can't say we had much in common. The fact is, there was a lot about Preston I just didn't get. Preston needed to stand out in ways I didn't understand—through his clothes, his hair, his music, his pets. (Ferrets, by the way.) He had a different way of looking at things than I did. I never thought it was because he was gay and I was straight. It's just that we were different. But now I wonder. How much of a different worldview do you develop because you're gay or straight? I'm going to find out. I'm going to become a student of gay life in America. This isn't about "getting lost or immersed in a strange lifestyle"—I have no interest in being a 56-year-old, overweight, straight man on the disco floor. I'll do this academically. I'll read. I'll talk. I'll see what I can see. I want to break through stereotypes and reach truths. I want to get closer to Preston.

Testing limits. "Six years ago, I was informed that there was an 84 percent chance I would be dead within 5 years. A lifelong nonsmoker, I had lung cancer. I lucked out: I'm a survivor. But back when everything looked bleakest, I surprised myself: rather than deciding to retire, I decided to throw myself into my work as president and creative director of an advertising agency staffed with more than 300 people I love. We'd been pretty successful, but I wanted us to go where few companies go—to build ourselves into an organization that could and would contribute in a positive, meaningful, and different way to society and to the lives of the people we touch. I want our company to be an agent for social progress. Advertising doesn't usually achieve that, but it has been done; Volkswagen ads did it in the '60s, Nike in the late '80s. I want our company to create work that has that kind of positive effect in the world. I also want our company to be a place with heart. A place that values and honors every part of an employee's life. I have made the pledge to myself and to our staff that we are committed to all this. We will go places no other company in our industry has gone. We will create something very, very special.

Take a leap of faith. "I guess—sadly—that racial tensions exist almost everywhere races coexist. But my hometown, Richmond, Virginia, has a special place in the history of America's racial conflicts. Wouldn't it be great if the old capital of the Confederacy could do something about those just-below-the-surface anxieties? If Richmond could do it, surely any city could do it. Civil rights gains in America have been great, of course, but they've been late and slow. And they haven't gone far enough. Nobody knows what else to do to make things better. It seems impossible. So too often we don't even try. I'm going to try. I had some thoughts about this a few years ago. I'm going to dust them off. I'm going to do something.

A self-indulgence. "I will spend significantly more time holding hands with my wife.

Testing limits (personal). "I was already overweight when my chemotherapy nurse told me I could eat anything I felt like eating while I was on chemotherapy because "nobody gains weight on chemotherapy." That was all the excuse I needed. Now I've got to lose a hundred pounds. A hundred freakin' pounds. I'll do it. I'll diet. I'll exercise. I'll do what I have to do. Gulp."

AN EX-CONVICT TURNED ARTIST

Anthony Papa has survived a very different kind of hardship. In 1984, Papa, who worked as a radio installer in the Bronx, was arrested with 4.5 ounces of cocaine and sentenced, under the strict new Rockefeller Drug Laws, to two jail sentences of 15 years to life. While in prison, he became an artist whose work attracted wide acclaim, and this led to his being granted clemency in 1997 by the governor of New York. Papa recently finished writing a book on his experiences, and his artwork can be seen on his Web site, www.15tolife.com. We asked him to share his List for Life.

Break new ground. "I want to change unfair laws such as the Rockefeller Drug Laws of New York State. I would try to do this by arranging a major conference open to the public, unlike the traditional secret meetings of government. Attending the conference would be lawmakers, the media, and families of those incarcerated—mothers, sons, and daughters. This would put a human face on the hidden tragedy of the drug war: nonviolent offenders serving draconian sentences for small amounts of drugs.

Express yourself. "I had an art show in 2002 that showed the portraits of those incarcerated and their children. In the middle of the installation stood a wall with photos of mothers separated from their children because of mistakes they had made in their lives. I wish I could have a traveling exhibit to visit every city in America and bring forth this message.

Shed your inhibitions. "When I went to prison, I was lost and desperate to overcome the negative environment. I discovered my talent as an artist. There was something mystical about sitting in a 6x9 cell. It made me look into myself, and I found a hidden talent. I then shared this discovery with others by starting an art class in Sing Sing Prison.

Test your limits. "My goal is to write a book that shows that people make mistakes in their lives and deserve to have second chances. In my case, I went to college while in prison—and received three degrees, including a master's degree.

Reach for the sky. "I would like to paint a gigantic public mural, for all to see, that captures the idea of breaking down walls that separate us from one another. It would be a magical painting. Once you looked at it, you would discover its message and would be compelled to pass it on to others.

Get lost. "My dream is to live in a beautiful exotic country like Brazil.

Living in an art studio surrounded by nature and creating art that can make a connection with others and share the message that life is beautiful."

LIVING WITH HIV

Dan Noonan, 36, is a community health planner for HIV services in the Chicago area. Dan has hemophilia, and about 20 years ago, he was infected with HIV through a blood transfusion. Today, he is a husband and father, also a "long-suffering unproduced playwright."

Here is Dan's list.

Get lost. "I would like to take a week where I do not plan ANYTHING. Hour to hour, I would only do EXACTLY what I feel like doing at the time. This goes for sleeping, eating, everything. Planning makes me feel secure, so this could be a little rough . . . I would like to do this once a year.

Face your fear. "I'd like to be able to donate my whole body to medical science (preferably after I'm dead). This is different from donating organs. In medical school, students basically shred cadavers bit by bit to learn about the human body. I think it would be a great way to help, because I know med students find it to be an extremely valuable process. And with my numerous chronic health conditions, I know the importance of good doctors. But I still have an irrational fear of doing this, and I haven't been able to sign on the dotted line yet and let myself be stripped away layer by layer.

Test your limits. "I would like to know how something mechanical works, like a car. From bumper to bumper, I want to know exactly how it is put together and how each system works to make the car run. I once heard a close friend comment, 'Dan has never given a moment's thought to how anything mechanical works.' It's true.

Take a leap of faith. "I would like to learn French well enough to travel alone in France.

Rediscover your childhood. "I would like to do or say at least one silly thing each day that makes my wife and son laugh. I have fond memories of funny, loving adults when I was a child, and my wife, Anne, remembers hearing her father make her mother laugh almost every morning. Unfortunately, it is going to be difficult to duplicate this exact experience because most mornings, my disposition is similar to that of a serial killer.

Express yourself. "I would like to have one of the plays I have written fully produced for a few weekends, even if I have to do it myself in my own basement, which looks like the only way it will happen.

Break new ground. "I'd like to make a full Thanksgiving dinner, all by myself, for my family. I just scrambled my first egg EVER for my son last weekend, so I have a ways to go.

Aim for the heart. "I plan to write letters, speak out, and do whatever I can to contribute to establishing universal health care in the United States. I can point to my own experience as a hemophiliac. Because my healthcare costs are so high, many employers, especially smaller companies, can't afford to hire me. And if people with bleeding disorders do get hired, they are often first to get laid off. The solution is healthcare that is not tied to jobs. If I can have a part in making this happen someday, then I can lay down and die in peace."

ASSORTED DREAMS AND DREAMERS

The following are excerpted highlights from the lists of various other interesting people we've gotten to know.

Alix Hartley, a top Hollywood agent with the Creative Artists Agency, has already tested her limits by climbing to the summit of Mount Kilimanjaro and has "gotten lost" by trekking with the Tuareg, a nomadic tribe of the Sahara known for wearing blue robes. Still remaining on Hartley's list: She wants to circumnavigate Mount Kalish, the holiest mountain in Tibet, and also plans to shed her inhibitions by bathing in the Ganges River.

Margaret Peot, a New York artist, wants to "get lost" by going to Japan and devoting a year to studying *shibori,* the ancient art of Japanese "tie-dyeing," with a master of that intricate craft. She says she "would learn a little of the language, live in the countryside, commute in to the city by rail, and have eel for lunch." She also wants to test her limits by learning to play the banjo and then recording a bluegrass song (perhaps the Stanley Brothers' "Will You Miss Me?").

Angela Aiello recently retired from her long-time job as an administrative assistant at age 65. She is now trying to "fulfill the many desires that there was never enough time for during my working years. I call them my PADs (pushed-aside dreams)." She recently fulfilled her first PAD when she visited a local wolf conservation center and went eye-to-eye with these creatures that have fascinated her all her life.

Stefan Sagmeister, a renowned international graphic designer who divides time between Austria and New York, recently took a "leap of faith" by choosing to work a year without clients, so that he could devote himself to design experiments (that is, to "break new ground" in his field). But Stefan wants to venture out in other ways, too: His list includes a plan to "drive a truck from the U.S. to Europe, through the Bering Strait going from Alaska to Siberia."

Doris Roberts, the award-winning actress who plays Marie Barone (Ray's mother) on the hit TV series *Everybody Loves Raymond,* reports that the top item on her list these days is traveling the world to try to inspire poor children. Having been named a U.S. cultural ambassador, she recently made her first trip in that capacity, visiting with teenagers in Costa Rica. "My message is, do not give up or give in, and do not take 'no' for an answer," she says. She hopes to take that message to kids in India next. Meanwhile, Roberts, 74, also plans to continue speaking out against ageism in the U.S. "It is the last bastion of bigotry in our country," she says. "There's no reason for it. Would you tell Picasso he couldn't paint any more, or tell Einstein we don't want your theories because you're too old?" And when it comes to testing her own limits, Roberts—who still attends acting class every week—is looking for a role that will stretch her. "People think of me as just being funny," she says, "but I'm also an actress and I'd love to take on some great dramatic role."

Michael "Nicko" McBrain is the drummer for the legendary heavy-metal rock band Iron Maiden. McBrain's dream is to put down his drumsticks and make a documentary film about an 82-year-old friend, Jim Marshall, who has been a big influence on Nicko's life and music. It's a way for Nicko to break new ground and aim for the heart, simultaneously. Also on his list: He plans to take a leap of faith by skiing in the Swiss Alps, something he's always been wary of doing for fear of injuring his drum pedal foot. "But I'm getting close to the point where I'm just going to do it," he says.

Robin Huffman, a New York interior designer, wants to test her limits by mastering "Tellington Touch," a technique for touching and handling animals to calm them (she wants to work on gorillas and lions). She also dreams of "getting lost" in the Sahara Desert in Niger during the Wodaabe tribe's annual Geerewol festival, in which, Robin explains, "stunning men are prized for their beauty and elegance." During the coming year, she plans to go to Kenya to paint murals in a children's hospital ward.

And on top of all that, she dreams of using her architectural skills to "break new ground" by building a cottage in the woods, off the grid and largely self-sustaining—possibly using recycled carpet tiles or abandoned tires as raw material. (But it still "has to be beautiful," she says.)

Kevin Roberts, the CEO of Saatchi & Saatchi, a global advertising giant, is focused on his native New Zealand: He wants to help create 100 start-up Sustainable Enterprises (in other words, enterprises that are environmentally responsible) in New Zealand, and would like to do so in Ireland, as well. He also wants to help reduce teenage crime in New Zealand through the Turn Your Life Around (TYLA) Trust, and he dreams of opening "the most fun, most-loved restaurant/bar in New Zealand."

LETTERS TO N.O.W.

For those still searching for a few more ideas, I thought I'd share (with permission of the writers) a handful of the hundreds of letters sent in to the TV show *No Opportunity Wasted.* I find something inspiring in each one of these.

Dear No Opportunity Wasted:

My dream is to put together my own burlesque troupe and put on a show. It would be a night of fun, frolic, music, dancing, girls, great costumes, and crappy comedy. I've been visualizing my show for years and have it all planned in my head. I've got all the talent lined up; I'd just have to say the word. All I'd need is to decide on the space where we would put the show on and organize the whole thing, which shouldn't be too hard, right? It would be great if you helped me make my lifelong dream come true. So what do you say, pick my dream!

—Marissa Gomez, Los Angeles

Dear No Opportunity Wasted:

My dream is to:

> *1. Become the oldest firefighter ever to complete U.S. Forest Service*
> *smokejumper school*
> *2. Become the only municipal fire chief ever to become a smokejumper*
> *3. Live this dream with my two sons who are both firefighters, becoming*
> *the only father and sons ever to become smokejumpers together*

As a fire chief in the Lake Tahoe area, we live with the daily threat of wild-
fire, and because of that, I have had the opportunity to fight wildfires of every
type and size for over 25 years. I have also participated as a member of an in-
cident command team, traveling to large fires throughout the West. At one of
these fires, I met another USFS fire chief from Florida. He told me the story of
how he came to be the oldest firefighter to become a smokejumper. After several
more days of fighting fire in mountain-goat terrain, he told me that when I re-
tire, I should go to the smokejumper academy and break his record.

—Brian Schafer, Lake Tahoe, California

Dear No Opportunity Wasted:

At the age of 30, I had my first and only child, Douglas. Born with a hole in
his heart, Douglas had open-heart surgery at the tender age of 3 months. Later,
we found out that he had other birth defects. The most troubling is that Dou-
glas was born without a portion of his brain. He struggles with motor skills,
speech, and thought processes.

Douglas is the light of my life, and I am blessed to be his mother. He is 8 years
old now and making lots of progress. He loves animals and oftentimes says he
wants to be a veterinarian when he is older. Here is where my dream comes into
view. I've read that there are many places that provide "dolphin therapy" for
special-needs children. I've always wanted to swim with dolphins since I was a
little girl. I never had the opportunity, but now my dream is to have Douglas

receive dolphin therapy. Unfortunately, the cost has been too great for my family to afford.

I can just imagine a relaxing summer day with my family when Phil Keoghan knocks on my door and asks if this is the Grinzinger home. I would have the biggest smile on my face! My son and husband's jaws would drop! All of us would fly to Key Largo and head straight to "Dolphins Plus" Marine and Mammal Research and Education Center. We would splash and swim with the dolphins all day. I realize that "miracles" may not happen with Douglas and the dolphin therapy. However, I would know in my heart that at least we tried!
—Janet Grinzinger, Missouri

Dear No Opportunity Wasted:

My dream is to organize the World's Largest Human Chain—America's Call for Peace on Earth. Imagine approximately 15 million Americans holding hands (I did the math) from the pier at Battery Park in lower Manhattan to the Pier in Santa Monica, California. Literally from sea to shining sea—all in the name of peace. If you have ever held hands with a group of people—around the dinner table, at church, or as a team—then you know the power of making that human connection. Not unlike electricity or other forms of energy, this human chain will physically connect people from just about every race, creed, religion, ethnic group, and color on Earth.

How will this work? A route has been selected; 2,796 Global Positioning System points have been assigned, which represent each mile from start to end; participants will go to a Web site and select a GPS point nearest them; you will be assigned a number between 1 and 5,635; and on the date of the event, all 15 million participants will get in line according to their number. The idea is for me to be the first person in line at Battery Park—then jump on a chartered jet and fly to the Santa Monica Pier and arrive just in time to be the last person in line!
—William Sancho, Miami

Dear No Opportunity Wasted:

My dream is to re-create a portion of a trip that my father, his brothers and sisters, and my grandfather took over 100 years ago. The trip was from Northeastern Oklahoma (then Indian territory) to Trinidad, Colorado. They traveled in a wagon train. My dream is to spend 1 or 2 days and 1 night on this trail in a covered wagon. I would like to take my son-in-law with me and also my grandson. He will be 8 years old and I will be 65 years old. These are the ages of my father and grandfather when they made the trip.

—Jesse Jones, Oklahoma

Dear No Opportunity Wasted:

My dream is to climb a Mayan pyramid . . . dressed in full drag as my character "Nuclia Waste." I would climb to the top of the Pyramid of the Magician (in Uxmal, Mexico), wearing my 5-inch white platform boots, lugging a boom box. I understand the pyramid is quite high and the steps were made for small Mayan feet. So climbing to the top could be quite treacherous. At the top of the pyramid, I would do a victory performance, lip-synching to "I Am What I Am." I have been wanting to do this for 4 years now, ever since I created my drag character Nuclia Waste. I almost got the chance to do this last year when I was on a cruise ship and we were supposed to port in Merida, Mexico. I even had a Mayan feather headdress made for the occasion. Except our cruise ship got fogged in at New Orleans. I never got the chance to live out my dream.

—David Westman, aka "Nuclia Waste," Denver

Dear No Opportunity Wasted:

I remember as a kid, looking through a photography book and seeing a photo of a man changing the red beacon light on top of the Empire State Building. I want to be that man. I'd love to be the guy that changes those bulbs high above the city. Maybe because you are the highest person in the city at that moment and you're only going to hear the wind. No city sound, no horns honking, no voices . . . nothing.

234

I was a constant tree climber when I was a kid, hence the nickname "monkey-boy" which has stuck with me for 25 years. To make this dream more interesting, I'd like to be able to change the red beacon lights on several well-known buildings/towers (Chrysler Building, Golden Gate Bridge). Maybe even make it a contest to see if I can change a bunch of lights, on different skyscrapers, within a given amount of time.

—Stephen Ross, Albany, New York

Dear No Opportunity Wasted:

Israel was my best friend to skate with since I was 12. We skated after school at the competitions, and we started to get sponsors together. In September, Israel moved to Little Rock, and I have no one to skate with after school. I miss him. There are other people, but it's not the same as when he was here. He calls almost every weekend and tells me about Little Rock. He has some people to skate with there, but they don't have any ramps. He really misses the team and all the fun times we had, too.

I have never been outside of California, and what I would like to do for my dream is go to Little Rock and surprise Israel. We have both heard all about the famous Louisville Skate Park, so I would like to take him there to skate. It is open 24 hours a day.

This is the good part of my dream. While Israel and I are skating in Louisville, the rest of the team, Lamonzo and Andrew, will be in Little Rock building a ramp for Israel. When we get back, he will see the ramp and the team will be together, and we will have a competition which I will win (I hope).

—Jeffrey Harris, age 17, Los Angeles

Dear No Opportunity Wasted:

My dream is to go back to Vietnam. In 1971, I was a soldier there with the Navy Seabees, a building construction branch. We were at a jungle region of the country called Ta Kou. We had a Howitzer blasting rounds out of our camp day and night, and I can't believe I'm still here. One of the reasons I believe I'm here is because of a massive Buddha statue that is lying on his side near the moun-tain road that we were building. I always told myself that I would return someday, find the place where I spent months blasting my way up the mountain, and climb up to see this huge statue.

When I flew out of Vietnam, I felt I left a piece of me behind—you would help me find that piece 32 years later. It would be so exciting to see if any of my camp is left. And I would be so excited to find the Buddha. But the adventure doesn't end there. I will also drive to Da Lat, where I have been writing to a girl. It would be so exciting to meet her, because she wants me to go and visit the Damri waterfalls where there are monkeys and birds living in the jungle.

It would be such a thrill to go back to Vietnam without an M16 rifle in my hand. I just thought of something else I could do. Because I can take a 70-pound box on the plane, I can deliver medical supplies to the Saigon hospital. I do a lot of facilities work for Vietnamese doctors here in San Jose, and they can get me the supplies. Wow—I'm so excited!

—Frank Harper, San Jose, California

I wish I had room to print more of these letters. More than that, I wish I could personally help bring all of these applicants' dreams to life. But my message to them, and all dreamers, is: Don't wait for me or anyone else to come knocking on your door. You've thought about this dream, you've envisioned it, you've written it down. Only one thing left to do: Start making it a reality.

And the same goes for every reader of this book. You've been given all the examples you need. Your list should be complete by now. And in the next and final chapter, we'll talk about what you should do with it.

12

LIVE LIFE N.O.W.!

L ET US ASSUME that you now have a completed list in front of you. (And if you don't, it's time to shut the book, put pen and paper in your pocket, get yourself to a tree house or some other secluded spot, and don't rejoin us until the list is done.) Because the main purpose of this book is to get you to write that list, my work is almost finished. Meanwhile, it may seem that *your* work is just starting—indeed, you have all these challenges staring you in the face now, and you haven't even begun to work on any one of them. But the truth is, you've already done the hardest part.

Think about it: You've narrowed down a world of endless possibilities into a manageable group of challenges that offer some of the best, most meaningful ways to bring your own dreams to life. Just making those eight choices represents a significant achievement, and one that most people never quite manage to do. And you not only made choices, you went further and made a commitment; you did this when you put it all down in writing. So that piece of paper in front of you is something to be proud of, and to treasure. Because really, it's more than just a piece of paper. It is your springboard to a new life.

Unless . . . you make the mistake of treating it like just another piece of paper. We all know that certain kinds of lists (and I'm not talking about grocery lists here but rather the more ambitious kind, such as New Year's resolutions and 5-year plans) are often written with good intentions, then set aside and ignored. These lists are put into a drawer somewhere. Or pushed to a corner of the desk, soon to be buried under other pieces of paper.

We're going to make sure that doesn't happen with this list, and here is how: We're going to make the list ubiquitous. It's going to be like Britney Spears used to be: hard to ignore, impossible to avoid. The first thing you should do is bring your list to the nearest copy machine and make 20 copies of it. But make the copies in different sizes—some at 100%, some reduced to 50%, and some as small as you can make them without losing legibility. Then take those copies and post them in high-visibility places. Obviously, there are any number of places in your house where you can tape the list. The refrigerator door is a rather obvious choice (though not the best, actually; things become invisible there). I happen to like the idea of putting the list inside doors you open regularly—inside the medicine cabinet, inside your clothes closet, or in the cabinet where you keep your coffee mugs (a list behind a door tends to surprise you, which is good). The tiny copies of your list can be affixed to the back of your phone receiver or (my favorite) taped to the back of your TV remote control. There should be at least a half-dozen places throughout your house where the list is posted. Then move outside: the dashboard or sun visor of your car, your bulletin board at the office, your locker at the health club.

Finally, take the remaining lists and give them out to a few close friends or relatives. As I've said previously, it's important to let people know that you are planning to do these things. They may be able to help you in some way that you can't even imagine. Or they may ask you nagging questions ("Say, how's it going with that list of yours?"), and that

Make Your Mark, But Don't Leave a Mess

As you venture out into the world, remember that wherever you go, you're a guest—and should behave accordingly. Respect the people and the cultures you visit, and do your part to ensure that pristine environments remain that way. I recommend following the guidelines of the Leave No Trace Center for Outdoor Ethics (www.lnt.org), a nonprofit group dedicated to promoting responsible outdoor recreation. Here are some of the group's basic principles.

- Travel and camp on durable surfaces; avoid disturbing wetlands and riverbanks.
- Dispose of waste properly. Pack it in, pack it out.
- Leave what you find. Examine but do not touch natural artifacts.
- Minimize campfire impacts.
- Respect wildlife. And don't feed animals in the wild.
- Be considerate of those around you. In particular, keep your noise level down. Let nature's sounds prevail.

can be a good thing. And who knows—you may inspire them to write their own lists, which means you can nag them as they nag you.

All of this may seem trivial, but it's not. When you're trying to do things that are out of the ordinary, trying to break the routine of your life, you need these constant reinforcements. I have been working on the *No Opportunity Wasted* dream for years—it was tough to sell the idea of the TV show, and even tougher to sell the concept as a book—and during the long haul, I wanted to make sure that this dream always remained at the top of my mind. One of the ways I did that was to order a customized license plate with the letters "NOW" on it. This was long before there was a show or a book or anything tangible; that license plate was the first tangible thing. And every day when I went out to my car, I saw that license plate and it reminded me that I had a dream to pursue. Even as I got swept up in lots of other jobs and tasks, the license plate helped keep N.O.W. alive.

My coauthor, Warren, used a similar strategy a few years ago when he set out to write a screenplay. He was afraid that, like so many writers, he would start the screenplay but never finish it. So he custom-ordered (at no small expense) a batch of baseball caps with the title of his screenplay printed on the front. He gave some hats out to friends, wore one himself occasionally, and kept some kicking around the house. The hats not only served as a reminder to him, they caused other people to ask about the screenplay. All of which helped push him to get it done. Both Warren and I were guilty of putting the cart before the horse when we made those premature hats and the N.O.W. license plate, but they served their purpose by giving us something tangible that we had to live up to and couldn't ignore. So if you feel you must, then by all means go beyond posting lists. Make yourself a special hat or license plate, give yourself a tattoo, or do whatever else it takes to keep your dreams in plain sight.

DECIDING WHERE TO START

Once you've posted and circulated your list, you must take some form of action on one of the items, immediately. Here I will reiterate the formula I originally shared in chapter 1: *Probability diminishes as procrastination escalates, ultimately yielding nothing (squared).* The more time that elapses between writing down a dream and acting on it in some way, the less likely it is that you will do it. With your finished list, it's critical that you take a first step on one of the items right away, to get some momentum going.

And it doesn't have to be item number 1 on the list, by the way. You shouldn't approach your list in a rigid numerical order, particularly as you're getting started. On the one hand, facing your fear can be an excellent challenge to begin with, for reasons cited in chapter 3 (for example, it can help you come to terms with fears that might inhibit you as you move on to other items on your list). But on the other hand, it may be that the particular Face your Fear experience you've decided on is one of the more complex and demanding challenges on your list—one that may require a lot of time to set up, or that may call for special conditions and circumstances. If that's the case, you may want to start with something on your list that is simpler and more immediately attainable so that you can get off to a fast start.

This is all part of taking an *opportunistic* approach to your List for Life. As you begin to act on that list, you should always factor in opportunity—and by that, I mean taking advantage of good timing, circumstance, available resources. Right now, at this moment in your life, it may be a particularly opportune time to try number 4 on your list. Maybe there are currently good deals on flights to that part of the world. Maybe your father is coming to town soon, and item number 4 involves him in some way. So the idea is to survey your list from top to bottom, and then decide where it makes the most sense to start.

IDENTIFYING RESOURCES

A big part of being opportunistic is identifying resources that are available to you. And often, the most important resource is people. As you study your list, look for the experiences that might involve other people you know. Do you plan to have certain people accompany you on some of these experiences? If so, bring those people into the discussion right away (unless you're planning to ambush them, of course). These partners represent a great resource in terms of adding brainpower, ideas, and personal contacts to the mix as you begin planning. Even if you're planning a go-it-alone experience, think about who might be able to help you—the uncle who has a cabin, the sister who's a travel agent, or even just the friend who's a great "idea" person. Talk to these people. I'm a big proponent of brainstorming, and I think it's something you should do right away in this process. Take a few people out for coffee or drinks, and tap into their ideas, suggestions, and enthusiasm.

Aside from people, other resources available to you might include time (When is your vacation period? What other blocks of time are available? Can you manufacture some free time?), your own expertise (take stock of the various skills and knowledge you have that may be relevant to each of the challenges on your list), and even raw materials on hand (if you know about some unused lumber somewhere and you want to build a tree house, find a way to tap into that resource). It comes down to asking yourself two questions: *What do I have?* and *What can I do?*

THE PLAN

Once you've identified your resources and brainstormed a bit, it's time to start laying out a specific plan for the first experience you're going to pursue. When I help people get started on trying to live out their dreams on the *No Opportunity Wasted* television series, I urge them to come up with a plan that is flexible and pliable, but one that is also clear in its vision. A good exercise is to start by trying to imagine and visualize the way your dream experience might play out, including all the stages and, in particular, the way you envision yourself at the end. If this were like a fairy tale—the best of the best—what would the experience be like? What would it feel like? (It's good to aim for the ideal, because that leaves room for inevitable compromises and scalebacks along the way.) If it helps, you should write down this description of how you see the experience playing out. Just by pushing your mind to visualize the details of an experience in this way, you've gained some clarity and taken an important first step.

Then, you should begin to get more practical. Plan out the actual steps that must be taken between now and the start of the experience in order to set it up: This includes people to be contacted, flights to be booked, and training courses to be taken. It can be helpful to set up "milestones"—little goals you can strive for, small victories along the way. Example: You might say, "Tomorrow I will make three phone calls to X, Y, and Z, to get the ball rolling." Three phone calls is a fairly easy and small first step. But it can be very important in terms of establishing momentum. Once you've made those calls, you've set something in motion. People begin to call you back. Concrete plans start to take shape.

Keep in mind that those first steps can be hard because you're battling inertia. You've got no momentum on your side. But as soon as you take those first steps, even if they're small ones, the dynamic begins to change. Now you are in motion and the forces of momentum are gathering on your side. What's more, you are now *invested* in the process. The more you invest, the more likely you are to keep going so as not to squander the investment. (You'll find yourself saying things like, "Well, I've put this much time in already, might as well keep going. Plus I've already told my uncle, so if I quit now, I'll never hear the end of it.")

Every step you take, with each small investment of time or effort, increases your momentum.

A big part of your planning and your investment in the dream involves doing your homework. We covered this a bit earlier in the book, but it's worth restating here: Preparation is important, necessary, and, quite often, rewarding in itself. It should be seen and embraced as part of the experience, not as a chore. Whether it's a matter of taking training courses or studying up on your own, the more you have

START YOUR ADVENTURE WITH A CLICK

Using the Internet is a great way to begin your journey before you even leave the house. Depending on what your dream is, you can probably tap into a search engine like Google to find almost any information you need. There are also several large, general adventure-travel Web sites worth mentioning as good starter points. They can show you what kinds of off-the-beaten-path trips are available. Some of the sites offer packages, some sell gear, and some allow you to communicate directly with adventure-travel experts. They're worth checking out, with one caveat: Most, if not all, of them are selling something, so factor that in as you turn to them for advice.

http://gorp.away.com: One of the biggest adventure-travel sites, with information on destinations and outdoor gear.

www.iexplore.com: You can book more than 3,000 different adventure-travel trips, offered by more than 130 tour providers.

learned prior to an experience, the better you will be able to enjoy and appreciate the experience. And, of course, the safer you'll be. If you're going white-water rafting in Costa Rica, you should do enough homework to know that you're going with a reputable company. I happen to enjoy that research process, and it's now easier than ever before because of the Internet. (I tend to assume everyone has Internet access, but if you don't have it at home, your local library does. And if you're not great on a computer, maybe your nephew is—this could be another

www.altrec.com: A complete source for outdoor gear, clothing, and equipment.

www.secondascent.com: If you're on a budget, this site offers secondhand outdoor gear at discounted prices.

www.rei.com/adventures: Books on all types of trips; also provides access to in-house adventure experts.

www.adventuretraveltrips.com: This is a directory and search engine linking adventure companies from around the world.

www.adventuretravel.about.com: Lots of articles and basic information on adventure travel, with a newsletter you can sign up for.

www.mountainzone.com: A clearinghouse of information on climbing, skiing, hiking, mountain biking, and anything to do with mountains; site also includes a trailfinder.

www.mtsobek.com: Since 1969, Mountain Travel Sobek has been a pioneer in adventure travel, particularly in small-group travel. The renowned adventure writer Richard Bangs has been one of the group's guiding leaders through the years.

case of using a resource available to you.) Whatever your dream may be, there is a good chance you can learn about it on the Web. Without knowing what your dreams are, I can't recommend specific sites, but I've tried to include a few general adventure Web sites to help get you started.

To my mind, the most important planning involves these aforementioned steps leading up to the experience: the cold calls, the Internet searches, the freeing up of time, everything that makes it possible for you to arrive at the actual experience. But once you begin to live out that experience, you may or may not want to follow a detailed plan. If your dream involves, say, traveling from coast to coast in Costa Rica, you might not want to be bound by an itinerary; perhaps part of the adventure is to work it out on the way. Keep in mind, though, that if you take this approach, you must be flexible: When you find that the special little hotel you wanted is unavailable because you didn't book it in advance, you must accept it and move on to another option. Some people can live that way, and others like to have things nailed down to every last detail. You have to decide what's right for you. (Though if you are one of those itinerary people, I do urge you to try—at least once, perhaps on your Get Lost experience—throwing away the hour-by-hour plans. Try just winging it and see how you like it. It may be a revelation.)

THE MOST IMPORTANT
THING TO PACK

After you've made the arrangements and taken the necessary first steps, as you're actually heading out the door on your first experience, make sure you've packed the most important thing to bring on any adventure—a sense of humor. If you have nothing but that, you will survive. Time and again on *The Amazing Race*, the most successful teams have used humor to help them get through the challenges of the journey.

Here's why it's so important: When you allow yourself to become angry and frustrated—over delays, bad weather, lost tickets, whatever— the brain basically shuts down. You stop thinking clearly. You lose your resourcefulness. It also has an effect on the way people around you interact with you. They tend to become less inclined to help you. But if you can avoid yelling or sulking and instead make a wry little joke about your misfortune, suddenly people will go out of their way to help. Of course, I know it can be difficult to control emotions in a bad situation. But try to keep reminding yourself of the following:

- Trials and tribulations are part of the experience; they're part of the climb up the mountain. Did you really think there would be no difficulties in that climb?
- Almost every difficult situation can be an opportunity. If you're caught in a storm with a random group of people, does this situation offer a chance to test your limits? And maybe bond with those people?
- Finally, remember that every difficult situation eventually becomes a badge that you will proudly wear. Tell the truth: Don't you always end up sharing your airline horror stories with other people? And we all want to top each other's horror stories: "You think that's bad? Listen to what *I* went through!" So whatever is happening at the time, remember: It's all fodder. You may even want to take notes.

I don't need to tell you to enjoy the experience, because I know you will. What I do recommend is that you savor the moments of the experience. Does that mean clicking an endless series of photos? Only if you love taking photos. Does it mean you should record it all on a camcorder? Probably not; you can get so wrapped up in recording an experience that you miss out on living it. Better to come out from behind your camera and face the experience, the people, and the world around you. (Diaries and journals are not a bad idea, though.) Mostly, just try to capture and freeze moments in your mind. Always be on the lookout for little N.O.W. moments that you can mentally document— those immortal moments that will become part of your life's highlight reel.

When you've completed an experience, celebrate. On the N.O.W. series, we encourage people to plant a flag in the ground, like an explorer conquering a new world. I encourage you to do likewise; you can use an invisible flag if you like. Or write your name in the sand. Or pee it into a volcano (yes, it's possible to do that, and in fact it's on my list).

Then come home and tell us all about it at the *No Opportunity Wasted* community Web site. And gather your family and friends to tell them firsthand about your experience. Don't make them sit through long videos or laborious slide shows. Bring the experience to life through your own stories. Share your discoveries. Convey your enthusiasm. Try to spread the philosophy of *No Opportunity Wasted*.

But don't spend too much time talking. The next adventure on your list awaits you.

WELCOME TO DREAM CENTRAL

It can be lonely setting out on a new way of life. But at www. noopportunitywasted.com, you can connect with others taking the same journey. When you've finished creating your List for Life, send it here and we'll register you on our database as an official N.O.W. dreamer, with your list posted on the site to help inspire others. Periodically, we'll highlight the lists we like best and send a *No Opportunity Wasted* prize to those whose lists are featured. The site is also a place to communicate with other dreamers—to share suggestions, pass along travel and adventure tips, ask questions, or just air your frustrations. And we want you, as our dreamers, to give us ongoing progress reports on experiences you have fulfilled and others you are setting out to fulfill. We want to know how you're doing as you journey along on this new road. Most of all, we want you to know that you're not alone. There are a lot of dreamers out there, and starting now, they have a place to congregate.

N.O.W.: Reader's Worklist/Contract

AGREEMENT made as of _____ 20__, between _____ (hereinafter "Subject") and himself/herself, to be considered a binding contract unless otherwise specified.

WHEREAS, Subject agrees to embrace the *No Opportunity Wasted* (or N.O.W.) philosophy, as well as the attitude and lifestyle encompassed therein;

WHEREAS, Subject shall not delay in embarking on said lifestyle, and shall not offer excuses pertaining to alleged lack of time, nor shall Subject issue vague promises to begin "later," or "next month," or some other future date;

WHEREAS, Subject has agreed to compile the following personalized list and to act on that list immediately, in any order that Subject sees fit;

NOW, THEREFORE, Subject agrees to commence doing the following:

1. (Face Your Fear) _____

_____

2. (Get Lost)_____

_____

3. (Test Your Limits) _____

_____

4. (Take a Leap of Faith)_____

_____

5. (Rediscover Your Childhood)_____

_____

6. (Shed Your Inhibitions/Express Yourself) _____

_____

7. (Break New Ground) _____

_____

8. (Aim for the Heart) _____

_____

Witnessed by: _____